THE JESUS MYTH

BOOKS BY ANDREW M. GREELEY

AND YOUNG MEN SHALL SEE VISIONS

THE CATHOLIC EXPERIENCE

THE CHANGING CATHOLIC COLLEGE

THE CRUCIBLE OF CHANGE

THE CHURCH AND THE SUBURBS

COME BLOW YOUR MIND WITH ME

THE EDUCATION OF CATHOLIC AMERICANS
(with Peter H. Rossi)

A FUTURE TO HOPE IN

THE HESITANT PILGRIM: AMERICAN CATHOLICISM AFTER THE
COUNCIL

THE JESUS MYTH

LETTERS TO NANCY

LIFE FOR A WANDERER

NEW HORIZONS FOR THE PRIESTHOOD

A PROFILE OF CATHOLIC HIGHER EDUCATION

RELIGION AND CAREER

RELIGION IN THE YEAR 2000

STRANGERS IN THE HOUSE

UNCERTAIN TRUMPET

WHAT A MODERN CATHOLIC BELIEVES ABOUT GOD

WHAT WE BELIEVE *(with Martin Marty
and Stuart Rosenberg)*

WHY CAN'T THEY BE LIKE US? ETHNIC CONFLICT IN AMERICA

THE JESUS MYTH

Andrew M. Greeley

Doubleday & Company, Inc., Garden City, New York

*To two men who in very different
ways made this book possible—*

Clifford Geertz and J. Michael Hartnett

CONTENTS

l'amour de Dieu, c'est folie . . .

—from the French Easter liturgy

NOTE

The word "myth" is used in the title of this volume in
a specific and definite sense. A myth is a symbolic story
which demonstrates, in Alan Watts' words, "the inner meaning of the universe and of human life." To say that Jesus
is a myth is not to say that he is a legend but that his
life and message are an attempt to demonstrate "the inner
meaning of the universe and of human life." As Charles
Long puts it, a myth points to the definite manner in
which the world is available for man: "The word and
content of myth are revelations of power." Or as A. K.
Coomaraswamy observes, "Myth embodies the nearest approach to absolute truth that can be stated in words."

Many Christians have objected to my use of this word
even when I clearly define it specifically. They are ter-
rified by a word which may have even a slight suggestion
of fantasy. However, my usage is the one that is common
among historians of religion, literary critics, and social
scientists. It is a valuable and helpful usage; there is no
other word which conveys what these scholarly traditions
mean when they refer to myth. The Christian would be
well advised to get over his fear of the word and appreciate
how important a tool it can be for understanding the
content of his faith.

THE FOUNDER OF THE FIRM

This is a book about the Founder of our firm, one Jesus of Nazareth. It is not a scientific biography, since we do not have the materials for such a biography. It is not an original theological work, since I am not a theologian. Even though it is based on the most recent research on the New Testament, it is not an exercise in New Testament studies, since I am not a Scripture scholar, either. All the book can claim to be is a series of reflections from the religious symbolism of Jesus.

To say that Jesus is a religious myth or symbol, albeit the most important religious symbol in the Western world, is not to deny him reality. There is nothing more real than men's symbols and myths. To say that Jesus is a symbol does not say that his life and message are legend. Quite the contrary, it is the very core of the myth of Jesus that his life and message were real historical phenomena; phenomena which, even though we perceive them through the theological understanding of the primitive church, still have powerful historical value in the strict sense of the word.

There was a time, not so long ago, when many scholars were persuaded that the story contained in the gospels was mostly a fabric of legends derived from the Hellenistic world to which Christianity had moved after the fall of Jerusalem. In particular, it was argued that much of the symbolism of Christianity was derived from the mystery cults which were contemporaneous with it in the fading world of Greece and Rome.

We now understand, however, that the symbolism of primitive Christianity is mostly Jewish, that the Christian "mysteries" owe very little, if anything, to the mystery cults of Hellenism, and that even the logos theme of St. John is more Jewish than Greek. Furthermore, we have also discovered that, while there may be an occasional similarity in language or theme between the Christian symbols and the symbols of pagan legends, the really striking thing is not the similarity between Christianity and the Orphic or Dionysian mysteries, but rather the immense difference. In dealing with the symbolism of Jesus of Nazareth we have to contend with a symbol that is drastically different from the other religious symbols of his own time or indeed of any time.

One hears it said frequently today that Jesus and his message are "irrelevant" to the problems of the modern world. The irrelevance of Jesus is not however a new discovery. He was irrelevant to his own world, too; so irrelevant that it was necessary for him to be murdered. The symbolism of his life and message was no more adjusted to the fashionable religious currents of his day than it is adjusted to the fashionable ideological currents of our day. Much has been made recently of the similarity between the message of Jesus as contained in the New Testament and the beliefs of the monastic Jewish sect which lived in the hills overlooking the northern end of the Dead Sea. Surely the Dead Sea community tells us much about the religious atmosphere of Palestine when Jesus appeared on the scene, but, as we shall note in a later chapter, the striking thing about the relationship between Jesus and the Dead Sea community is not the similarity but the great diversity. Some of the categories of expression, some of the religious tools were the same, but the content of the message was profoundly different.

The symbolism of Jesus, then, was as much out of harmony with his own time as it apparently is with ours. One reflects at length and in depth on the symbolism because despite its apparent continuous irrelevancy it has still managed to survive and, indeed, become the dominant religious symbolism for a substantial segment of the human population. One hears that today the influence of the Jesus symbolism has finally run its course. But even announcement of the decline of the influence of Jesus of Nazareth has been made repeatedly since the soldiers rolled the stone across the door of the tomb. Nonetheless, somehow or other, the symbolism has managed to survive. One is therefore rather well advised to be skeptical about the demise of Christianity. It becomes, therefore, appropriate to try to probe the meaning of the symbolism of Jesus if only to learn whether despite its obvious irrelevancy it might still say something important about the human condition.

The religious reflections on the symbolism of Jesus contained in the present volume result from the fact that some time ago I became "hooked" on New Testament studies. In my work in the sociology of religion I have been more and more influenced by the writing of Professor Clifford Geertz, who thinks of religion as a set of symbols which provide man a "meaning system" that can answer his fundamental problems about the interpretability of the universe. The "templates" which guide the behavior of animals are for the most part provided by innate instincts, but man has rather few instincts and is capable of surviving in the world not because he is endowed with an elaborate system of instincts but because he is able to evolve culture; that is to say, a series of meaning systems with which he can interpret and organize his life. Man's religion is the most fundamental of his meaning systems because it is one which provides an answer to the most puzzling and basic questions about the meaning of existence itself. In Geertz's words, "Without religion; that is to say, without a basic meaning system, it is not merely that man cannot interpret the meaning of problems like death and suffering and unexpected events, but he finds himself threatened with an uninterpretable universe. Without religion, interpretability collapses and man is immersed in chaos."[1]

Geertz's point is not that every man believes in God or that every man requires the sacred or even that every man agonizes frequently during his life over problems of ultimate interpretation and interpretability. His point is rather that most of us need, at least implicitly, some sort of rough and ready answers to questions of whether life has meaning,[2] of whether good triumphs over evil; or evil, good; of how the good man lives; of whether the really real is malign or gracious; and of whether man is capable of establishing relationships with the real. Our religious symbols contain, frequently in highly poetic form, the ultimate meaning system or interpretive scheme which we use to cope with these questions.

My interest in the writings of Geertz began with a conviction that those who, like Dietrich Bonhoeffer or the younger Harvey Cox, argued that secular man no longer needed a religion, completely misunderstood the nature of the human condition. An anthropologist, Geertz discovered in his work in Java and Morocco that modernization and "secularization" of these societies, far from eliminating religion, made religious needs more acute, precisely because the meaning questions now became very explicit and conscious. Bonhoeffer is quoted less frequently, and Harvey Cox has gone far beyond the walls of the secular city, and I found myself increasingly faced with the question of what

---

[1] Clifford Geertz, "Religion as a Cultural System," in *The Religious Situation*, Donald Cutler (ed.). Boston: Beacon Press, 1968, p. 668.
[2] Is Macbeth right when he says that life is a tale told by an idiot, full of sound and fury, signifying nothing; or is Teilhard de Chardin right when he says something is afoot in the universe?

it meant to say that Christianity was a symbol system or an interpretive scheme. What were the "privileged" Christian symbols and what sorts of answers do they provide to the fundamental questions of interpretation and interpretability of the universe? Was it possible that both Christian theology and Christian controversy had become so involved in peripheral issues that the role of Christianity's principal symbols as providing interpretation of the universe had been overlooked?

There isn't much doubt that Jesus of Nazareth is the central symbol of Christianity. His life and message as contained in the gospels either would contain the main themes of the Christian interpretive scheme or these themes would not be found anywhere. But at this point I found myself in a rather surprising position. Even though I thought I knew what the Christian answer would be to the basic questions about the meaning of the universe in Geertz's sense, I was hard put to link those answers with the person and life of Jesus. In my mind, and I suspect in the minds of most of my contemporaries, the symbol of Jesus has become so encrusted with piety, theological controversy, and ecclesiastical triumphalism that it means very little. Piety is clearly outmoded. Controversy seems to pertain to issues no longer of much moment and were, perhaps, never anything but peripheral, and triumphalism seems designed almost deliberately to obscure Jesus behind Byzantine robes and ritualism.

It must be understood that a Catholic clergyman of my generation learned practically nothing about New Testament studies in the seminary—or Old Testament studies either for that matter. We were led to believe, though perhaps not deliberately or explicitly, that most New Testament scholars were agnostics or skeptics or "liberals" who were basically concerned with denying the uniqueness or the authenticity of Jesus and quite possibly both.[3] While my generation of Catholic clergy has been able to assimilate

[3] Unquestionably, at one point in the development of New Testament studies such a charge had some validity.

the impact of Old Testament literary criticism, we have not turned our attention to New Testament criticism. Indeed, the little we heard about it (usually from some of the younger clergy who had read a book or two or heard a lecture about Rudolf Bultmann) persuaded us that when the New Testament critical scholars were finished there was nothing much left of Jesus and not much in the way of historical basis for our faith.

I must make it plain that I was not especially concerned that my faith would be in danger if I wrestled with the writings of the New Testament scholars. Faith is not rooted in scholarship, and anyone who adjusts his fundamental orientation toward the universe so that it fits what university faculty members are currently writing simply has no notion of either the mutability of academic thought or its extreme limitations as a means of coping with reality.

However, I had heard enough about the conclusions of those scholars who had ruled out the possibility of a realistic search for the "historical Jesus" to conclude, quite wrongly as it turned out, that there was not much to be learned from them about the content of the Jesus symbol. I would later discover to my dismay that those friends of mine who had read a book or two and announced that we could know nothing about the historical Jesus were twenty years out of date and that the post-Bultmannians had a great deal to say about the historical Jesus.

But I was ready to accept Bultmann's unhappy compromise. It seemed to me to be sensible to settle for the symbolism which the early Church in its New Testament writings perceived in the Jesus phenomenon if one could not break through to the phenomenon itself. With this in mind, I turned somewhat skeptically to the New Testament literature and began to plow through the writings of men like C. H. Dodd, J. Jeremias, Rudolf Bultmann, R. H. Fuller, E. Kasemann, N. Perrin, W. Marxsen, A. J. B. Higgins, T. W. Manson, G. Bornkamm, with increasing fascination and enthusiasm.

I am not engaged in a sociological analysis of Jesus of
Nazareth, but I did begin with the perspective of the sociology of religion. Nor did I begin seeking confirmation
for a faith about which I had doubts, much less seeking
arguments to convert others to my faith (I have a hunch
that usually these last two enterprises are the same). On the
contrary, I approached the work of New Testament scholarship with respect for the abilities of the men who engaged
in it, with increasing fascination for their brilliance and
skill, and in search of deeper understanding of the faith to
which I was firmly committed. I now propose to share my
reflections on this literature with the readers of this book,
because it seems to me that the fears and misunderstandings
which most educated Catholics have toward New Testament studies deprive them of insights which could be of
extraordinary importance for their religious life. As Professor Hans Küng has put it:

> The background to the gospels, and in particular the first
> three synoptic gospels, is not legend and speculation, but
> living experiences and impressions, reports handed down
> about the living Jesus of Nazareth. If not directly, at least
> through the evangelists' testimonies of faith we can hear
> Jesus himself speaking. Anyone who comes to these docu-
> ments with essential rather than peripheral questions and
> puts them seriously rather than casually, will receive answers
> which are remarkably clear, consistent and original; answers
> which are obviously not just the product of a chance coin-
> cidence of various theological versions of the truth, but
> which—however much occasional details may seem historically
> dubious—speak to us with the original words of Jesus.[4]

The myth about New Testament studies that is widespread among the Catholic clergy and educated laity—and

[4] Hans Küng, *The Church*, trans. by Ray and Rosaleen Ockenden.
New York: Sheed and Ward, 1967, p. 44.

not merely among those of us over thirty-five—have not progressed much beyond the understandings of A. Harnack or A. Schweitzer. We are more or less convinced that what the critical studies have concluded is that Jesus was an itinerant ethical preacher making no special claims to being a messiah, much less God's son, warning of the imminent end of the world, and paying with his life for the revolutionary implications of his ethical preaching. He had no intention of founding a church. The signs that he was supposed to have worked were made up by his followers. The prophecies he made were derived after their fulfillment instead of before. The resurrection was an extremely dubious event. The Gospel of St. John was produced under powerful gnostic influence. The concept of mysteries in the writings of St. Paul shows the influence of the Greco-Roman mystery cults. The virgin birth was a Hellenistic idea absorbed rather late in the day from pagan religions, and most of the words and deeds reported in the New Testament were piously fictional creations composed by the early church.

This summary of New Testament research, which I believe many Catholics accept as accurate, corresponds to what some writers were saying at one period in the development of the New Testament studies. They began with an assumption of a closed universe in which only those things that could be verified by empirical science could be considered as legitimate objects of human knowledge. The rationalists, the skeptics, the empiricists had their day in New Testament studies just as they did (and do) in most other scientific disciplines.

I am asserting that the thrust of the New Testament studies in the last two decades has gone far beyond the debunking skepticism practiced by some authors in days gone by. Most of the elements of the caricature described above were simply inaccurate. Jesus was not basically an ethics teacher at all. He apparently resolutely refused to set a time limit for the complete fulfillment of the Kingdom. He did not found the church in the sense of setting up a formal organizational model, but he left no doubt as to how the community of his followers were to behave. Even though he may have been executed because he was suspected of being a political revolutionary, he was not especially interested in the political issues of his time. At least some of his prophecies were clearly made before the events occurred. The tradition of Jesus as a man who performed marvels is so primitive and so powerful that some writers say the only historical explanation possible is that marvels did occur. St. John's gospel was not gnostic; it was written before gnosticism began and was basically Jewish in its orientation. And St. Paul's concept of history owed practically nothing to the pagan mystery religions. Finally, we can be historically certain that the early Christians had a profound experience of Jesus as still alive sometime shortly after his death. Historical science cannot say what the exact nature of these visions of Jesus was, and only faith can say what they mean; however, the fact of the experience cannot be questioned.

But I was to discover something much more important. When the "post-Bultmannians," by their rigorous and very skeptical methods of form criticism, finally got that body of material which they think can be attributed to the historical Jesus, we do not find obscurity and uncertainty but rather a basic teaching and a fundamental self-understanding of incredible clarity and power. While the theological reflections of the early Church on the person and teaching of Jesus are of immense importance to us, it is still useful to follow the post-Bultmannians on their project of stripping them away and getting back to that which can beyond reasonable doubt be attributed to Jesus himself. For when the symbolism of Jesus stands forth, unadorned by the reflections of the early Church, he is even more challenging than when he is obscured by the theological problems and concerns of primitive Christianity. Jesus was not an ethical teacher or an apocalyptic prophet. He did not think of himself in such a way and did not behave as either rabbis or prophets behaved. His self-understanding and his message were unique, original, and startling. It is small wonder that he shocked and frightened his contemporaries and that they would not accept what he said. It is also small wonder that we have done our best to obscure the shocking nature of the symbolism of Jesus ever since.

It is not my intention in the present book to summarize the work of the New Testament scholars. Rather, I propose to offer religious reflections based on my reading of their works. Anyone who wishes to pursue their work in the original can certainly do so on their own. (He would be well advised to begin with Gunther Bornkamm's *Jesus of Nazareth*.) I will occasionally attempt to summarize some of their conclusions as a basis for my own reflections, but these summaries will necessarily be brief and lacking in the complexity of much of the work of these scholars. I will limit myself for the most part to reflections on material which many of the post-Bultmannians confidently think comes from the historical Jesus. I do this not because I doubt the merits of the theological reflections of the early Church as contained in the books of the New Testament, but because I think it is a useful religious experience to reflect on the very core of the symbolism of Jesus. It is worth noting that the methodology of New Testament criticism is to include in the corpus of "historical" material only those passages which can be established as certainly historical beyond any reasonable doubt. It does not follow that a historically doubtful passage is certainly unhistorical; it simply is that its historicity has not been proven. Thus, most of St. John is not included in the certainly historical category because methods have not yet been discovered by which the scholars can confidently separate the various layers of tradition to be found in that highly complex gospel.

One should not assume that the New Testament scholars

are in complete agreement among themselves as to what material can confidently be said to be historical. There are lengthy and complicated debates, for example, over whether Jesus actually referred to himself as the Son of Man, and there are also debates over the extent to which Jesus explicitly applied to himself the suffering servant themes from Deutero-Isaiah. I am not qualified to make any judgments on these controversies. Jesus certainly seemed to have been reluctant to apply *any* titles to himself. However, there does seem to be general agreement that his attitude, his behavior, and his preaching were such that the use by the early Church of religious categories such as the Suffering Servant and the Son of Man to describe him was certainly valid. It ought to be noted that the thrust of these controversies tends to swing back and forth. What one generation of scholars assumes to be true beyond all doubt another generation calls into serious question. Such is the nature of the academic enterprise in every discipline. This is not to say that nothing is certain in New Testament study, but one must be wary of staking his religious commitments and convictions on the scholarly opinions currently in fashion. I know of one priest who left the Church because (so he claimed) his analysis of St. Mark convinced him it was impossible to believe in the myth of the empty tomb since it was so clearly a legend created by the Hellenistic Jewish community out of which Mark's gospel came. I was not competent then and I am even less competent now to follow the logic of his argument; however, the most recent scholars are now currently convinced that Mark was Palestinian rather than Hellenistic in its origins. I suspect that the priest in question will not return to the Church despite the fact that the scholarly opinion he used to justify his departure has been discredited. It is worth keeping in mind that positions on specific controversies are quite likely to change in any academic discipline from year to year, and that these controversies exist in a different order of knowledge and meaning than does one's ultimate interpretation of the universe, or at least they should exist in different orders of meaning.

A number of other observations about New Testament studies from the point of view of an outsider may be pertinent:

1. The intellectual capabilities of many of these men engaging in this field of scholarship are immense, even awesome. The skills, for example, that have gone into the recreation of the original Aramaic text of the "Our Father" are very impressive indeed.

2. Unlike most other practitioners of the social and historical disciplines, the Scripture scholars seem to have what Thomas Kuhn calls "paradigms" in his book *Structure of Scientific Revolutions*. Paradigms for Kuhn are statements of the nature of the problem which define clearly the context within which scholars can work. Once a discipline constructs a paradigm, immense and rapid progress can be made in puzzle solving. Form criticism and the quest for the historical Jesus seem to have provided precisely such a paradigm for New Testament study. However, as Kuhn notes, paradigms bring problems, and one of them is that those working within the paradigm are so caught up with the fascination of puzzle solving that they are quite unaware of issues which may not be stated in the paradigm. I find myself, for example, just a little bit surprised that most of the extraordinarily brilliant New Testament scholars seem unaware of the profound religious implications for our own time of the work in which they are engaged. (Joachim Jeremias is one outstanding exception to this stricture.) The concluding paragraphs of their books will occasionally provide a note of faith and piety, but beyond this they do not seem inclined to go.

3. For the English-speaking reader the work of New Testament scholars is made more difficult to understand because so much of it is done in Germany, and the German

professorial style of discourse is obscure at best (even in good translations). It becomes even more opaque when it is mixed, as in many of the post-Bultmannians, with doses of Heideggerian existentialism. However, despite the complexity and the obscurity and passion for minute technical detail, as well as the occasional arrogance of their work, anyone seriously interested in deepening his understanding of Christianity can ill afford to ignore the work of the New Testament scholars.

Let me make it clear for whom I am writing this book. First, I suppose I am writing primarily for myself, to clarify and deepen my own understanding of the meaning of the life and teaching of the Founder of our firm. Second, I am writing for all those like me who are trying to deepen their understanding of the faith to which they are committed in this disturbing era of change and confusion. I will not "defend" Christianity from the attacks of skeptical critics, nor do I propose (as a reviewer of one of my other books suggests) to reassure any "troubled" middle-aged Christians. (That reviewer, I am afraid, would have deemed anything other than a complete rejection of Christianity to be directed at those unfortunates in the middle years.) I certainly do not propose to try to explain Christianity to the agnostic secularist who has been labeled "modern man." It is not my intention to persuade the "young" that Christian symbols are "relevant."[5] Nor, finally, do I wish to argue with those members of the clergy for whom radical skepticism has become a personal stance excusing them from thought, inquiry, personal maturation, and religious commitment. I surely do not wish to deny the importance of any of these groups in modern society, but I assert that the position all of them take, each in its own way, rules out on

[5] Professor Mary Daly tells us that many of the young do not find New Testament symbols relevant. I rather doubt the representativeness of Miss Daly's sample, but if some members of the younger generation are so shallow and superficial as to dismiss symbols that have shaped human thought for two millennia without investigating deeply the meaning of such symbols, that is their problem and not mine.

a priori ground the necessity and even the possibility of trying to determine what Jesus means.

If this volume is any use at all, it will be limited to two groups of people: (1) Those Christians who wish to understand the core of their faith more deeply and to think about the implications of that faith for our particular segment of time and space. (2) Those non-Christians who are curious as to how the core of the Christian message is understood by one Christian social scientist living and working in the secular academic world.

Will we be able to conclude that Jesus is relevant? I think if we put quotes around that much abused word "relevant" and restate the question to say, Does the message of Jesus respond to contemporary intellectual and social fad? Then we will assert that Jesus is certainly not "relevant" today, no more than he was in his own time. If, on the other hand, the question is stated, Does Jesus throw down a challenge which has profound implications for men of every era? The answer is that Jesus is most certainly relevant and will be until the human race grows tired of pondering the meaning of life.

CHAPTER 2

JESUS AND HIS TIMES

Perhaps one of the reasons for the many controversies that have raged over Jesus of Nazareth is the difficulty in classifying him. For some, he seems a simple ethical preacher; to others, a mystical prophet; to others, an eschatological visionary; to yet others, a political revolutionary; and to still others, the founder of a church. It is not merely the different presuppositions that we bring to our study of Jesus that create the confusion. He is a hard man to categorize. He does not seem to fit into any of our neat labels, and this problem of figuring out where exactly Jesus stands is not a new one. Even in his own time he puzzled most of his contemporaries. In the concluding pages of his *Sayings of Jesus*, T. W. Manson summarizes Jesus' paradoxical behavior.

> His hearers were amazed by the authority with which He spoke. He dominated the crowds, and He was, without ever striving for mastery, easily the Master of His band of disciples. Yet He constantly insisted that He was the servant of all, and as constantly demonstrated the genuineness of that strange claim. . . .
>
> The religious authorities were horrified by the freedom with which He criticised doctrines and practices hallowed

by centuries of pious observance. Yet He was wont to go
to the Synagogue on the Sabbath; and He enjoined the
healed leper to do what Moses commanded in the matter
of his healing. . . .

Respectable people were scandalised by the freedom and
familiarity of His intercourse with the disreputable. He
was nicknamed 'Friend of publicans and sinners.' Yet the
quality of the friendship was determined by Him, not by
the publicans and sinners. . . .

The rank and file of the Jewish nation were estranged
in the end by His lack of patriotism. Yet He wept over
the impending fate of Jerusalem; and He was executed as
a political agitator along with two rebels against Rome. . . .[1]

In other words, Jesus went about providing answers to
questions that no one was asking and refusing to answer
the questions everyone thought important. He resolutely refused to permit himself to be part of any of the principal
religious or political currents of the environment in which
he lived. One can imagine that a frequent question people
asked about him was, "But where does he really stand?"

Palestine was in chaos when Jesus arrived. The Herods
presided over what was little more than a Roman puppet
regime. The Temple priesthood, somewhat influenced by
Hellenistic thought, co-operated with the occupying power
to preserve a little bit of their own autonomy. Political
revolutionaries were engaged in never-ending plots often
exploding into rebellions before, during, and after Jesus'
life until the final destruction of the Temple of the Jewish
nation. The Pharisees, an unofficial group of zealous laymen, were popular religious innovators who attempted to
regulate all human conduct by appeal to the Torah. The
Essenes and similar groups (including the community on

[1] T. W. Manson, *The Sayings of Jesus*. London: SCM Press, Ltd., 1964,
pp. 344–45.

the banks of the Dead Sea) shared with the Pharisees a zeal for the law, but, unlike them, emphasized the priestly element in the Jewish religion and, also unlike the Pharisees, felt it necessary to withdraw from the mainstream of Jewish life. The scribes were scholars of the law and obsessed with trivial debate over the interpretation of the letter of the law. The principal popular religious themes were either messianic or apocalyptic. To fulfill messianic hopes, a royal offspring of the house of David was expected to drive out the Romans and restore the political kingdom of Israel. In the apocalyptic strain an eschatological son of man was awaited who would introduce the kingdom of peace and plenty and prosperity for all. The messiahs, it was thought, would triumph with miraculous political and military victories; the Son of Man would arrive in the midst of cosmological marvels. For almost all the inhabitants of Palestine, the political and religious situation was intolerable. The past was superior to the present, and a much better future was eagerly anticipated. Pharisees, Essenes, Zealots eagerly awaited a better world, whether it be messianic or apocalyptic; and Jesus satisfied none of them.

The Pharisees were appalled at his casual disregard of the law and his vigorous condemnation of their moral self-righteousness. The Zealots could find in his preaching no promise of success in political revolutions. The Essenes were undoubtedly horrified by his proclamation of a kingdom for all men. Those who expected a political messiah were disillusioned when Jesus refused the claim that he was such a messiah and would have no part of the schemes to make him king. And finally, those who expected an eschatological apocalypse were told that they would see no signs from heaven and that they would hear from Jesus no guess as to when the last days would be fulfilled. In other words, Jesus rejected the titles, the categories, the theories, and the aspirations of all religious movements of his time. He did preach a kingdom, but it was a kingdom not of this world;

he did announce an eschaton, but it was one quite free from cosmological signs and wonders. Instead of insisting on the old law, he proclaimed a new one. Instead of extolling the uniqueness of the Jews, he preached Good News for all men. Small wonder that when the chips were down he found himself quite without friends or allies.

Without stretching the comparison too far, we can see that many of the religious ideas and movements in Jesus' time have their counterpart in our own day. The Sadducees, the corrupt, politically minded heirs of the ancient church, were an Establishment. The Pharisees were liberal reformers filled with self-righteousness and zeal. The Essenes were perfectionists, who had withdrawn from a corrupt society to build the new and more perfect world of their own. The Zealots were revolutionaries who believed that drastic political action would provide salvation from the injustices they saw all around. Those who expected a messianic kingdom are not unlike contemporary Marxists who think that new forms of political and social organizations will make the world a better place in which to live. And, finally, those affected by the apocalyptic spirituality were not too dissimilar from our own revolutionary utopians such as Professor Charles A. Reich and the other admirers of Consciousness III.

I am not, however, trying to argue that our time is more like the time of Jesus than other epochs in human history. My point is, rather, that the religious and political currents in Palestine in the time of Jesus represent certain fundamental themes that are reasonably typical of the human condition. The names may be different, but the Pharisees and the Sadducees and the Zealots and the Essenes are always with us and so are those forms of popular piety which sees salvation in political revolutions or the dawning of new paradisal ages. Reformers and revolutionaries, puritans and perfectionists, dreamers and defenders of the old order have always sought to find support for their positions in the teachings of Jesus, but he eludes their grasp just as effectively as he eluded the grasp of the movements in the currents of his own time.

To the Pharisees and the Sadducees, to the Essenes and the Zealots Jesus responded in effect by saying that they were asking the wrong questions and using the wrong categories. It was necessary, of course, as they all said, that God's will be done, but the will of God meant something rather different to him than it did to those who questioned it. As Manson puts it:

> For Pharisaic Judaism it was holiness and righteousness as revealed in the Law. For those Jews who nourished their souls on the Apocalyptic literature, there was added an intenser assurance of a Divine power that would destroy evil and vindicate righteousness, and that right early. For many the Kingdom of God meant the downfall of Rome and the exaltation of Israel to world-dominion. For Jesus the will of God is primarily the forgiving, reconciling, redeeming love of God. And being what it is, it must express itself in a Divine act for men rather than in a Divine demand upon men; though this demand follows inevitably upon the act.[2]

The answer was not a satisfactory one, not to the Essenes, the Pharisees, the Sadducees, the Zealots. It said nothing about purity or zeal for the law, or the upholding of the priestly tradition, or the restoration of the kingdom of Israel, or the beginning of the messianic or apocalyptic age. It said in effect that none of these questions mattered very much and what counted rather was God's forgiving love, but to that his hearers shook their heads in dismay. You couldn't restore a kingdom with God's redeeming love, nor could you protect the law from those who violated it, or

[2] *Ibid.*, p. 345.

maintain the dignity of the priestly tradition. It was no help in getting rid of the Romans, and it certainly didn't seem likely to lead to any reform of Jewish religious life. As a matter of fact, there wasn't much you could do with the message of Jesus at all.

Except believe it, and that was too easy and too difficult. It was too easy because it didn't involve fulfilling minute regulations or taking the field in combat against the Roman barbarians. It was too difficult because it meant depending on God rather than on oneself, and nobody was about to do that.

Neither then nor now.

Much has been made, particularly in the totally irresponsible articles by Edmund Wilson in the *New Yorker* magazine, on the similarity between Jesus and the separatist Jewish community of Wadi Qumran on the shores of the Dead Sea (a group which may or may not have been the same as the Essenes which the Jewish historian Josephus mentioned). That there are some similarities in vocabulary and category is not to be denied. The discoveries at the Wadi Qumran have made an immense contribution to our understanding of the religious atmosphere at the time of Jesus, but few responsible scholars today would argue that Jesus was part of the community whose members spent so much time bathing themselves in the sun-drenched rocks overlooking the Dead Sea. In his pamphlet, "Jesus and the Wilderness Community at Qumran," Ethelbert Stauffer notes nine differences between Jesus and Qumran. These differences nicely illustrate just how much at odds with his own day Jesus really was.

1. The Qumran community was heavily clerical; priests played a larger role there than in any other Jewish community of that time. But in the life and ministry of Jesus there is no reference to the priestly tradition.

2. The wilderness community was almost compulsively committed to ritualism. Jesus, on the contrary, argued that purity was internal rather than external.

3. The monks in the wilderness community were required "to love all the sons of Light and hate all the sons of Darkness," but Jesus insisted that we must love all men.

4. The Qumran sect was deeply involved in revolutionary militarism. Jesus argued that all that take the sword shall perish by the sword.

5. The Qumran community was obsessed with the minor details of the Jewish calendar. Jesus completely ignored the calendar controversies.

6. The wilderness community was committed to secret teachings and traditions. Jesus, on the contrary, insisted that he had spoken publicly for months and years and had said nothing in secret.

7. The Qumran community expected two messiahs: the kingly one from the house of David; the priestly one from the house of Aaron. Jesus, on the contrary, is completely unconcerned about genealogies and not very much occupied with messianic questions.

8. The Qumran sect was intentionally critical of Jerusalem priesthood and the Temple cult, claiming that it was illegitimate, deviant from the proper hereditary line of the priesthood. Jesus, on the contrary, took part in the Temple celebration and, while he was critical of the abuses, made no comment at all on the question of priestly genealogy.

9. Stauffer summarizes the differences between Jesus and the wilderness community with the rather startling assertion that they would have murdered Jesus as readily as the Pharisees and the Sadducees.

In addition to the manifest differences and certain readily admitted points of contact between Jesus and the spirit of Qumran, are there also antitheses? Is there anywhere a genuine "either/or" which is a life-and-death matter? I answer that there exists at least one major antithesis between Jesus and the spirit of the Qumran sect . . .—the attitude toward the Torah. By the Torah I mean the Mosaic law, as recorded in the five books of Moses and as found in its central formulation, the Ten Commandments. I contend: had Jesus fallen into the hands of the Wilderness sectarians, they would have murdered him as ruthlessly as did the Pharisees. For in the climactic period of his ministry, Jesus opposed the spirit of the Wilderness sectarians just as relentlessly as he did the spirit of the Pharisees.[3]

The wilderness community was even more rigid in its insistence on the law than Jerusalem either in its Phariseeic or Sadduceeic manifestations. The Torah was the measure of all things, and a man who breaks the Torah cannot be a man from God. And as good a measure of the importance of the law are the regulations of the Sabbath. In Stauffer's words:

The Sabbath laws were considerably more rigorous in Qumran than in Jerusalem. However, not only did Jesus altogether reject this heightening of the law; what is more, he fundamentally repudiated the Mosaic Sabbath law itself. For this reason there could be no fellowship between Jesus and Qumran, no understanding, no tolerance. There was simply no place for Jesus in the world of the Wilderness sect. Had he sought such a place, had he fallen into the hands of the Wilderness sectarians, according to their logic and exegesis of the Torah they would have condemned to death the rebel against the Sabbath in Qumran; they would have had to condemn him—just as it actually was done in Jerusalem.[4]

The early Church chose to use many of the categories of Jewish thought—Son of Man, Messiah, Suffering Servant—to

[3] Ethelbert Stauffer, *"Jesus and the Wilderness Community at Qumran,"* trans. by Hans Spalteholz, Facet Books Biblical Series—10. Philadelphia: Fortress Press, 1964, pp. 20–21.
[4] *Ibid.*, pp. 33–34.

describe the ministry of Jesus, but what is striking about the way these categories are used is that if we compare the Christian use of them with the pre-Christian use, whether it be among the sectarians at Wadi Qumran or in popular Jewish piety, the content of the category undergoes drastic change. The early Church claimed that Jesus was the Messiah, Son of Man, the Servant, but the words now meant something rather different, and necessarily so, because if Jesus was a messiah he was unlike any messiah that had previously been expected, and if he was an apocalyptic son of man, the signs and wonders and the eschatological age introduced by them were drastically different, and if he was the servant of God, the *ebed* Yahweh, he infused service with a meaning that was certainly not understood by those who had pondered over the implications of the later chapters of Isaiah.

It would appear that Jesus deliberately avoided titles because the titles that were popular in the religious atmosphere of his time could only lead to a distortion and misunderstanding of his message. When the early Church fell back upon these titles because it needed some kind of category, because it had to have some kind of theological concept to explain its experience of Jesus, it was forced to modify drastically the content of the titles so that they meant something quite different from what they did to the compulsive hand washers of the Wadi Qumran and the zealous puritans of Jerusalem.

The point of all this is that Jesus was appallingly unique. He was a man of his time—born in Judea, raised in Galilee, speaking Aramaic, understanding Hebrew, honoring the central tenets of the Jewish law, and dying under the unjust administration of Roman justice. But his style, his message, and his challenge ignored rather completely the critical religious and social controversies of the day and, indeed, quite explicitly aimed to transcend such controversies. The symbolism which Jesus' life and message represent is profoundly original and quite unlinked to the social and cultural epoch in which he lived or, indeed, to any social or cultural epoch.

Jesus came to preach a simple, profound, but quite straightforward message, one that jarred his audiences and led them to conclude, first of all, that he was irrelevant and, second, that he might very well be dangerous. His message was rejected by all the leading groups of his society, and because he persisted in it it was necessary to get rid of him.

And if he was irrelevant to his own society, he was far more irrelevant to the deterioration of Greek culture and Roman government that constituted the frightful hodgepodge of the Hellenistic world with its cults, its sects, its mysteries, its obscure philosophies, and its endless political intrigue. Perhaps the principal difference between the reception Jesus would have received in Rome as compared to the one he received in Jerusalem is that in Rome it would have taken much longer to decide that he was an enemy of the people.

It is my contention that nothing much has changed. The revolutionaries, the establishmentarians, the liberal reformers, the utopians, the philosophers, the cultists, the mystics, and the schemers of our era are no more impressed by Jesus of Nazareth than were their counterparts in his own time. He was irrelevant then; he is irrelevant now. He was dangerous then; if people really began to take him seriously today, he would be perceived as dangerous now. Stauffer says he would have been condemned to death at Qumran as much as at Jerusalem. In our more humane era we might dispose of him by trying to turn him into a television personality rather than by executing him. But if we would not slay Jesus, we would at least imitate our predecessors and try to ignore him.

Some of the more enthusiastic Catholic political revolutionaries would have us believe that the gospel of Jesus legitimates their cause (I shall say more about this in a later chapter). They are quite wrong, of course. Jesus did not advocate political revolution; neither did he condemn it. But he argued that human happiness and human salvation would be achieved, if they were achieved at all, by other means. However, in a sense deeper than politics, Jesus was indeed a revolutionary. Indeed, even more radical than the revolutionaries. His message was distorted; he himself was disposed of because he was a threat to everyone in sight, left and right alike, and he would continue to be misunderstood, misinterpreted, and distorted down through the ages for precisely the same reason.

The rather simple, straightforward, and shocking message which Jesus came to bring was an attempt to redirect the course of human history, to change the style of human behavior and transform the nature of human relationships, and to reorder human life. It was an attempt which was not notably successful in his own time and has not achieved very much success since then.

It may not be legitimate for Jesus of Nazareth to ask that we accept his message, that we believe his Good News, but surely he has a right to insist that we listen to what he really says and that we respond to what in fact he is telling us and not to the misrepresentation and distortions that our own concerns bring into his message. As I say, he has a right to ask this, but, on the basis of performance, past and present, his expectations that his rights will be honored cannot be very great.

In the last paragraph of his book *The Sayings of Jesus,* Professor Manson summarizes the Good News.

The essence of the Gospel is that Jesus—His life and death and victory over death, His ministry, His teaching— Jesus is the divine act, the fulfilment of God's redemptive purpose, the incarnation of the Kingdom of God. The ministry of Jesus is no mere prelude to the coming of the Kingdom, nor even a preparation for it: it *is* the Kingdom at work in the world. His ethic is no mere 'interim ethic' to bridge the gap between the present and the future: it is the will of God which, whenever and wherever the Kingdom comes, is done on earth as it is in heaven. God was in Christ reconciling the world unto Himself. It is probable that the key to the teaching and the ministry of Jesus, and indeed to the whole New Testament, lies in a single phrase, which expresses, as perfectly as words can, the supreme interest of our Lord, that for which He lived and died, for which He endured hardship, loneliness, and obloquy, that to which He gave His whole undivided devotion—not 'the Law and the Prophets,' not 'the Kingdom of our father David,' but 'the Kingdom of my Father.'[5]

So the question we must face then is, What is the kingdom of his father that Jesus preaches?

[5] Manson, *op. cit.*, p. 345.

CHAPTER 3

THE KINGDOM IS AT HAND

The phrase "the kingdom of my father," with which we ended the last chapter, has been heard so many times down through the course of nineteen hundred years that we have lost any sense of what a bombshell it was when Jesus first uttered it. All three words are important: "kingdom," "my," and "father." In this chapter we will reflect mainly on the first word, and we shall use the word "kingdom" because it is the one most familiar to us from the Scriptures. However, we must note that the word meant something rather different to those who first heard it than it does today. Not only were they steeped in the eschatological writings of the Scriptures but they also had some sense of the power and the majesty of the king, a sense which is lost today when most of our kings have little power and most of our men of great power do not choose to call themselves kings. The word "kingdom" might be more appropriately translated as "reign" (as C. H. Dodd translates it) or "power," or perhaps the same idea might be conveyed if we mentally note that whenever Jesus says, "The kingdom of God is at hand," it can be understood as meaning, "The promise of God is about to be fulfilled." It was the notion of fulfillment of an age-old promise which most excited the crowds when Jesus emerged for his brief ministry of preaching. Something staggering, immense, overwhelming was about to happen, for

God's age-old promise of redemption was now being fulfilled.

We can summarize the core of Jesus' message around
five propositions:

1. One must change one's life, for the kingdom of God
is at hand.

2. The day of salvation has dawned.

3. The principal sign of the kingdom and its salvation
is God's loving mercy.

4. No matter how the kingdom is opposed, and no matter what happens to it, the kingdom will triumph.

5. Since now we have heard the Good News of salvation
of the triumph of the kingdom, we must rejoice.

The message is very simple and, through repetition down
through the centuries, has become trite. But its simplicity
and its triteness should not obscure for us the fact that the
message responds to the most basic and agonizing question
that faces all who are part of the human condition: Is
everything going to be all right in the end? Jesus' response
was quite literally to say, "You bet your life it is." Or, to
put the matter only slightly differently, to the question of
whether life was ultimately a tragedy or a comedy, Jesus
replied with the absolute assurance that it was comedy.

1. The theme of Jesus' preaching was indicated in the
first chapter of St. Mark, fourteenth verse, and in the fourth
chapter of Matthew, seventeenth verse. Gunther Bornkamm
quotes the two texts and observes:

> "Now after John was arrested, Jesus came into Galilee,
> preaching the gospel of God, and saying: 'The time is
> fulfilled, and the kingdom of God is at hand; repent and
> believe in the gospel'" [Mk. i. 14ff.]. "From that time Jesus
> began to preach saying, 'Repent, for the kingdom of heaven
> is at hand'" (Mt. iv. 17). With these words the first two
> evangelists sum up the whole message of Jesus. Each does
> so in his own language: Mark clearly in the language of

the first Christian mission, Matthew in the language of the
first Jewish-Christian community, which shuns the name of
God, saying "kingdom of heaven" instead of "kingdom of
God". There is no difference in substance: God's kingdom
is near! That is the core of Jesus' message.[1]

The word in Greek for repent is *metanoia*. It means more
than giving up sinful habits. It means, rather, the transformation of the basic structures of one's life. The intervention
of God in history which had been expected for ages was
now about to occur; indeed, was in the process of occurring.
Old styles of life, old forms of religious behavior, old attitudes and dispositions must be cast aside because they
are no longer pertinent. We simply cannot continue as we
have in the past. The whole situation has changed. Jesus'
hearers were in no doubt as to what he meant. They knew
the passages from the Psalms about the kingdom of God.

"All thy words shall give thanks to thee, O Lord; and all
thy saints shall bless thee!
They shall speak of the glory of thy kingdom, and tell of
thy power,
to make known to the sons of men thy mighty deeds, and
the glorious splendour of thy kingdom.
Thy kingdom is an everlasting kingdom, and thy dominion
endures throughout all generations" [Ps. 145: 10–13].
"The Lord has established his throne, in the heavens; and
his kingdom rules over all" [Ps. 103: 19].[2]

And if they were in any doubt, Jesus quickly clarified
the issue for them. In the scene in the synagogue of Naz-

[1] Gunther Bornkamm, *Jesus of Nazareth*. Trans. by Irene and Fraser
McLuskey with James M. Robinson. New York: Harper & Row, 1956,
p. 64.
[2] Quoted in Bornkamm, *Ibid.*, p. 64.

areth, which St. Luke uses as the introductory theme to his theological reflections on the message of Jesus, one sees Jesus standing in the synagogue reading an eschatological passage from Isaiah:

> The spirit of the Lord has been given to me,
> for he has anointed me.
> He has sent me to bring the good news to the poor,
> to proclaim liberty to captives
> and to blind new sight,
> to set the downtrodden free,
> to proclaim the Lord's year of favour.

Jesus then quite calmly rolled up the scroll, gave it back to the attendant, and sat down (as was appropriate when one was preaching in the synagogue), and, with all eyes fixed upon him, serenely announced, "Today this scripture passage is fulfilled in your hearing." Foolish arguments would rage down through the ages about whether Jesus thought he was the messiah or not. What he thought of himself (which we will turn to in a later chapter) is less important than what he thought was happening. He clearly thought that the messianic age, the reign of God's kingdom, the eschatological banquet, call it what we will, had begun, and it had begun in and through him.

2. "Now is the day of salvation." In responding to inquiries from the disciples of John the Baptist, Jesus (Luke 7:22, Matthew 11:3) once again, somewhat freely, quoted Isaiah. The blind see; lame walk; lepers are cleansed; deaf hear; poor have the gospel preached to them. Jesus is not necessarily claiming that all these events have occurred, but that once again the "Day of the Lord," the day of salvation, has begun. The old age is finished; the turning point in human history has arrived; a new era has begun. The dream of Isaiah has become a reality. In Professor Joachim

Jeremias' words, "Salvation is here; the curse is gone; paradise has come again." It is time not to repair old garments with new cloth but to put on new robes. It is time when new wine must be poured into new wineskins. It is a time of a new harvest and a new vintage, and the intoxicating wine of salvation is now available for all men. (Noah planted a vine after the Deluge, Israelite spies brought a bunch of grapes from the Promised Land, and Jesus creates a superabundance of wine in Cana in Galilee, each act indicating a new age is beginning.) As Professor Jeremias summarizes it: "The old garment and the new wine tell us that the old is passed, and the New Age has been ushered in."[3]

This turning point in history is described in a number of different poetic images. A new shepherd is sent for the lost sheep. He gathers his little flock around him. A physician has come to the sick. A messenger comes with a summons to a wedding feast. A head of the family gathers the family around him and invites guests to the table. An architect builds a new temple. A king makes a triumphal entry. These images indicate the same theme: a decisive turning point has occurred. And Jesus has come to announce it.

3. The intervention of God in history is not one of punishment and judgment but rather of mercy and love. This is what is especially good about the Good News. Salvation is sent to the poor and Jesus has come as a savior for sinners. Four of the parables of Jesus emphasize this theme: the parable of the Prodigal Son (or, as Professor Jeremias calls it, the parable of the Father's Love), the parables of the Lost Sheep and the Lost Drachma, and the parable of the Good Employer. In the parable of the Prodigal Son, the emphasis is not on either the sinfulness of the son or the jealousy of his brother but on the love of the father. In the parables of the drachma and the sheep that are lost,

[3] Joachim Jeremias, *The Parables of Jesus*. Trans. by S. H. Hooke. Charles Scribner's Sons, 1963, p. 118.

the emphasis is on the utter foolishness of hunting down one lost sheep or spending so much time on one mislaid coin. Only a crazy shepherd or a foolish housewife would act so absurdly, just as only a slightly demented father would shower honor on him who was a wastrel. Finally, only an employer whose generosity had caused him to take leave of his senses would pay to those who had worked only one hour a whole day's wage.

Men have always suspected or at least hoped that God might be good, might even love us. The message of Jesus was not new simply because it vigorously confirmed that suspicion. The novel element in his Good News was that God's love was so powerful that it pushed Him to the point of insanity. God's passion for his people is so great that he dispenses with the normal canons of discretion and good taste in dealing with us. The Loving Father does not even give the prodigal son time to finish his nicely rehearsed statement of sorrow. The son has barely begun before he is embraced, clothed in a new robe and propelled into a festive banquet. The woman taken in sin is not required to express her sorrow or promise amendment. Before she can say anything Jesus sends her away with forgiveness. *L'amour de Dieu est folie* as the French Easter liturgy puts it.

We are scandalized by such behavior on the part of God. Why does he not behave with more dignity and respectability. If we were in his position we would have heard out the prodigal son and then told him to come back in a few weeks when we had made our decision. And we would have taken every precaution to make sure the adultress really was not planning on dashing back to the arms of her lover. Nor is our sense of scandal new. Apparently the story of the sinful woman was left out of the early versions of the gospels because, even though it was part of a very ancient tradition, it described a standard of leniency that was shocking to the strict moralists of primitive Christianity. They had already begun to try to remake God into the stern judge that they thought he ought to be. The stern judge might be foreboding, but at least he isn't embarrassing. The trouble with the God that Jesus claimed to represent is that he loves too much.

The parable of the Good Employer is especially interesting when one ponders the fact that there was a rabbinical story with which Jesus' audience was certainly familiar that was quite similar to it. But the point of the rabbinical story was that the workers who came at the last hour worked so hard they accomplished more than those who had come at the first hour and actually deserved to be paid the whole day's wage. But in Jesus' version of the story, the emphasis is not on the hard work of those who came at the end but rather on the generosity of the employer. As Professor Jeremias observes, "Thus in this apparently trivial detail lies the difference between two worlds: the world of merit, and the world of grace; the law contrasted with the gospel.[4]

Jeremias notes that the parables of Jesus were generally tools of controversy used to defend his Good News against the attacks of those who would not accept it.

> It was not to sinners that he addressed the Gospel parables, but to his critics: to those who rejected him because he gathered the despised around him. . . . Again and again they ask: 'Why do you associate with this riff-raff, shunned by all respectable people?' And he replies: 'Because they are sick and need me, because they are truly repentant, and because they feel the gratitude of children forgiven by God. Because, on the other hand, you, with your loveless, self-righteous, disobedient hearts, have rejected the gospel. But, above all, because I know what God is like, so good to the poor, so glad when the lost are found, so overflowing with a father's love for the returning child, so merciful to the despairing, the helpless, and the needy. That is why![5]

[4] *Ibid.*, p. 139.
[5] *Ibid.*, pp. 145–46

We must not pass over these parables quickly because we have heard them all before. We may not understand fully the dizzy incredibility of their meaning. Jesus is saying in fact that God's love and mercy are so generous that similar generosity in humans would be deemed madness. God's generosity in human affairs would be a sign that a man had become irrevocably demented. It is not merely that he has set up an accounting system in which a considerable amount of credit is deposited on our side of the ledger; it is also that he has in a moment of insane generosity thrown away the account book entirely and provided us with a checkbook full of signed blank checks.

4. The kingdom of God will certainly triumph. Professor Jeremias describes four "contrast-parables" (contrasting the beginning with the end) as expressing Jesus' confidence concerning his mission. The parables of the Mustard Seed, the Leaven, the Sower, and the Patient Farmer are all part of "the great assurance." The emphasis in all four is one of the inevitability of process. The mustard seed is planted and the processes of nature are such that it becomes a tree no matter how small the seed. Similarly, the tiny bit of leaven initiates a process of fermentation which will certainly transform all the dough. The sower casts his seeds on the ground and, despite the perils to which they are exposed, they nonetheless bear fruit. The farmer plants his crop and waits patiently, knowing that there is nothing more for him to do until the inevitable natural process produces the harvest. Not only is the Good News being announced, but the certain triumph of the Good News is being guaranteed absolutely. It is as certain as yeast transforms dough; as the seed grown into a tree; and as the crop comes to harvest. Nor does the certainty, in the final analysis, depend on the strength of human opposition or the weakness of human faith. God has intervened to begin the New Age, and no matter what we do it will continue. We can no more stop it than we can stop the sun rising in the morning.

5. It is therefore necessary for us to rejoice. The kingdom is like a treasure that someone finds in the field. He is so delighted with it that he sells all he has to buy the whole field. All the way to the real estate office and all the way back, the man bubbles with joy because he knows what a splendid find he has come upon. Similar is the man who finds a pearl in the market place. It's a terribly expensive pearl, and he realizes upon examination that it is a priceless find, worth far more than is being asked for it. Even if he has to sell all he possesses to buy it, it is still easily worth the cost. The pearl is far more valuable than everything he possesses and more. Norman Perrin summarizes the joy and surprise theme of these two parables:

The original form of these parables, then, has a double element: surprise and joy. They both speak of a man going about his ordinary business who is surprised by the discovery of a great treasure, and, in this respect, they reflect the sympathetic observation of the men of first-century Palestine that we claim is so strong a feature of Jesus' parables. In a land as frequently fought over as ancient Palestine the chance discovery of valuables hidden for safe keeping in some past emergency was by no means unusual, and every peasant ploughing his field must have had some such secret dream. Similarly, pearls could be of fabled worth, and every merchant whose business took him to far places must have speculated upon the chance of stumbling across one such pearl. So we have the secret dream suddenly and surprisingly fulfilled, and the overwhelming joy that then seizes the man and determines and dominates his future activity. The analogy is clear: so it is with the Kingdom of God. A man can suddenly be confronted by the experience of God and find the subsequent joy overwhelming and all determinative.[6]

6 Norman Perrin, *Rediscovering the Teaching of Jesus*. New York: Harper & Row, 1967, p. 89.

One must of course realize the extent of the treasure; one must grasp what the pearl is really worth. And when one has gained insight into the immense value of that chance finding, then no cost is too great, no inconvenience too serious to prevent obtaining the treasure. Indeed, the cost and the inconvenience are minor because in any rational calculation the treasure is worth far more. The man who sells all his goods to obtain the treasure does not think he's making any sacrifice. Quite the contrary, he knows he has stumbled on an extraordinarily profitable transaction; hence, he rejoices at the thought of the payoff.

Again we are forced to note the extreme simplicity of the message of Jesus. An old era is done. God is intervening to begin a new age. It is an era of incredible generosity. One must change one's life in order to benefit from the generosity, but so great is the payoff in accepting the abundance of the new age that our *metanoia* ought to be one not of sorrow and sacrifice but of wonder and rejoicing.

This message speaks to the most fundamental questions a man can ask: Is reality malign or gracious? Jesus replies that it is gracious to the point of insane generosity. Is life absurd or does it have purpose? The reply of Jesus is that not only does it have purpose but that God has directly intervened in human events to make it perfectly clear what the purpose is. What is the nature of the Really Real? Jesus' response is that the Really Real is generous, forgiving, saving love. How does a good man behave? The good man is a person who is captivated by the joy and wonder of God's promise. In the end, will life triumph over death or death over life? Jesus is perfectly confident: The kingdom of his Father cannot be vanquished, not even by death.

Jesus is saying that in the end it will be all right, that nothing can harm us permanently, that no suffering is irrevocable, that no loss is lasting, that no defeat is more than transitory, that no disappointment is conclusive. Jesus did not, as we shall see in a later chapter, deny the reality of suffering, discouragement, disappointment, frustration, and death, but he simply asserted that the kingdom of his father would conquer all of these horrors, and that God's generosity was so great that no evil could possibly resist it.

The message of Jesus, the Good News of the kingdom of his Father, deserves to be accepted or rejected for what it is: an answer to *the* most fundamental questions a man could ask. If we are to reject it, then let us reject it because we believe that evil triumphs over good, that life is absurd and is a tale told by an idiot, that the Really Real is malign, and that only a blind fool would believe that things will be all right in the end. For it is on this ground that we must accept or reject Jesus, not on matters of papal infallibility or the virgin birth, or the stupidity of ecclesiastical leaders, or the existence of angels, or whether the Church has anything relevant to say about social reform.

But the contemporaries of Jesus did their best, nonetheless, to avoid the issue. Jesus confidently announced that in the end all would be well, that a new age had dawned, that God was intervening in human history, and that the only appropriate response for us was to be delirious with joy. His audience did not say, "Yes, we believe you," or, "No, we think you're a fool." They rather said, "What about the cotton-pickin' Romans?" or "When are you going to produce the apocalyptic sign?" or "Why aren't you and your disciples within the Jewish law?" or "Which side do you take in the various legal controversies?" Jesus replied by saying that the Romans were not the issue, that the law was not the issue, and that cosmic miracles were not the issue. God's insanely generous love for us was the issue, and, in the face of that fact, the Roman and the Torah became peripheral. But his listeners stubbornly refused to concede that the Torah could possibly be peripheral or that the Roman domination of Palestine could possibly be a marginal question. The Torah and Rome—these were the relevant problems—and what did Jesus have to say about them? But, once again, Jesus responded that he had not come to discuss the law, nor had he come to challenge the Roman Empire. He had come to bring Good News that the Really Real was love, and to demand from men joy and response to that love. Sober, hardheaded, realistic people in his audience simply shook their heads. Why did he not address himself to the really critical questions?

But it was not merely those in his audience who ignored the point. Since Jesus first appeared on the scene to announce that the day of salvation was at hand, we have elaborated vast theological systems, we have organized a worldwide church, we have filled libraries with brilliant scholarship, we have engaged in earth-shaking controversies; we have done battle with all kinds of political tyranny; we have engaged in crusades, inquisitions, renewals and reforms; and yet there are still precious few of us who go about with the same kind of joy as does the man who has found buried treasure or who responds to the baffled happiness of the prodigal son showered with gifts by a father who has every reason to ignore him.

One can imagine what the dismay of Jesus was like. He came to bring the best news that man had ever heard, and, no matter how many different ways he stated it, nobody seemed to hear him. They were so concerned with their own petty fears, ambitions, and causes they simply did not seem to be able to grasp the plain and obvious content of what he said. But perhaps after a time it became clear to Jesus that in one level of their personalities they most certainly understood what he said; they pretended not to understand precisely because they realized the full implication of his Good News and understood the staggering *metanoia*. that would have to occur in their lives if they should take him seriously. For if everything was going to be all right in the end, then there was nothing left to worry about. One of course had responsibilities and obligations. One could not ignore the political, economic, social, or cultural world, but all of these terribly seductive human activities would be seen in a very different light. In fact, they might even be understood as games, games which the players knew they would certainly win. Jesus was asked about the Romans and about the law and about the cosmic signs because his audience did not want to face what life would be like if Jesus was right. They refused to listen to what he was saying not because it was burdensome, not because it was threatening, not because it was a vision of gloom and doom punishment, but because it was too spectacularly good, much too good, in fact, to be true. Jesus was rejected and ultimately executed not because of greed or ambition or fear, but, rather, because of cynicism. If there is any prophet more obnoxious than a prophet of doom, it is a prophet of joy.

It was cynicism, pessimism, and despair which defeated Jesus and continues to defeat him. So precious few of even those who claim to be his followers live lives that would lead one to suspect that they had indeed discovered a treasure in the field or had spotted a pearl of great price in the market place or, to use a somewhat more modern simile, a long-lost Rembrandt painting. Not very many Christians live lives of men who have been intoxicated by the eschatological wince of a new age. Quite the contrary, the average Christian is every bit as gloomy and sober as his non-Christian neighbors. Not many Christians go about with the bright eyes and the singing heart that were characteristic of the prodigal son. The typical Christian's eyes are downcast and his heart is heavy and dull. Only a few Christians live with the serene confidence that the triumph of goodness is as certain as the fermentation of dough by yeast. The typical Christian is at least as anxious as his non-Christian neighbor.

Many young Catholics think it is the height of fashion to say that Christianity isn't any different from good humanism, and even such a distinguished scholar as Father Gregory Baum seems astonished to discover that there are many good, generous, and helpful people in the world who are not Christians. Sometimes I suspect that both the young people and even Father Baum are not fully aware of how much modern secular humanism is merely Christianity in another guise. However, the important point that I think they miss is that Jesus made no claim to preach a gospel that was "different." His message was not a new attempt to define the good or the true or the beautiful. It was not a revelation of some deep substantive truth that men had not understood before. He was not a gnostic providing a secret way to wisdom. The gospel is not to be compared to the Koran or the Book of Mormon. There is but one secret that Jesus wished to reveal, and it was what man had always rather hoped was true: Reality is gracious. Jesus merely went one step further and said: "Reality is love. The kingdom of my Father is the kingdom of love, and all you have to do is accept that kingdom and joyously receive His love."

If the Christian is to be different from other men, it is not because he believes certain creedal propositions, or because he follows certain norms, or because he engages in certain ritual activities, or because he takes certain stands on social action issues. What marks the Christian off against everyone else is that the Christian is, in Brian Wicker's words, "The humanist who is sure of the ground on which he stands." The Christian knows that God is Love, that the Really Real is insanely generous in his affection toward us, that it will be all right in the end. The Christian may, of course, express his insight in certain propositions. He may believe that certain moral behavior is appropriate to him. He may engage in certain ritual acts. But the really important thing about him is that his confidence and joy transfuse everything he does.

But to the enthusiastic young Catholic who has suddenly discovered that there are people in the world who are not Catholic and wants to know how Catholics are different, one can only point out that by no means everyone in the world is willing to say, in Teilhard de Chardin's words, "Something is afoot in the universe." Not everyone in the world is willing to give himself over to ecstatic joy because he believes he has found the pearl of great price. Not everyone is willing to live life as though he has discovered a treasure whose richness will never diminish. Indeed, the irony is that not even most Christians are willing to live in such a way.

He who accepts the gospel of Jesus rejects nothing that is good in the world, turns his back on no human endeavor, runs away from no human problem, but he asserts by word and deed that there is nothing to fear, nothing to worry about, nothing over which to be dismayed. What he does is much less likely to distinguish him from others as the way he does it. The way he does what he does is the way of the man who has found the buried treasure.

So the modern searchers-after-relevance say to Jesus of Nazareth, "But what do you have to say about peace?" And Jesus replies to them, "My Father loves you." They say to him, "What is your position on the race question?" And he responds, "You ought to rejoice over my Father's love." And they say to him, "What do you think about the ecological crisis?" And he answers, "Nothing can stand in the way of my Father's love." And the young apostles of relevance shake their heads in dismay. Clearly this strange Jewish preacher is completely out of it. He doesn't understand the issues at all. What in the world does God's generous love have to do with peace or ecology or race?

When I try to summarize Christianity, as I have in the previous paragraphs, some people have said to me that I am merely promising to those who suffer, "pie in the sky when you die." But such an answer shows little insight into what Jesus was talking about. He was not simply preaching the existence of heaven or an afterlife in which the good would be rewarded or the evil punished; he was rather saying something more basic and fundamental. There was not the slightest taint of cheap consolation in Jesus' message. He did not deny the reality of suffering or death; he simply asserted that God was Love and that love triumphed in the end. He did not say that injustice was to be quietly accepted. He did not say that suffering was to be overlooked or that pain was to be denied. He did not say that death was not a terrifying reality. Rather, he addressed himself to something much more elemental and asserted that, despite suffering, despite injustice, despite misery, and despite death, everything would still be all right in the end. Because his Father was love.

We have said repeatedly in this volume that the message of Jesus was irrelevant in the sense that it did not address itself to the problems that his contemporaries thought pressing—and no more does it address itself to the problems deemed relevant today. And yet in a deeper sense the answers of Jesus were shatteringly relevant in his time and our own. For despite all the social progress we have made since A.D. 30, distrust, suspicion, hatred, injustice, misery, fear are as pervasive in the world today as they were in Jesus' own time. It has not dawned on us that a man's fundamental view of the nature of reality can have a profound effect on his ability to cope with social and human problems. Jesus did not deny the existence of injustice, much less did he excuse his followers from concern about the problems of the human condition. He simply insisted that they seek first the kingdom of his Father with the confidence that all other things will be added to it. What would have happened if the crowd believed Jesus? What would happen if we believed him? What if cynicism and distrust, suspicion, fear, and hatred began to melt away? What if a rapidly increasing proportion of the human race did believe in the fundamental reality of his love? Probably the only answer to this question is that we don't know because it hasn't been tried. But one can say with a great deal of confidence that it certainly would not hinder the solution of social problems, and at this stage in history it ought to be clear to us that every enthusiastic social movement the world has known has broken up on the rocky shores of human apathy, cynicism, and fear. The naïve conviction of some of the youthful radicals that they are the first ones to be concerned about injustice merely demonstrates how little history they know. And their disillusionment when their bright visions are frustrated—as every bright vision before them—ought to be an indication to them and to their middle-aged admirers that crusades based on self-righteousness, scapegoating, and compulsory virtue (imposed on others) never work. Something new and far more profound is needed in the way of transformation. Yet man stubbornly refuses to recognize that his enthusiasm, his passion, his vision, is no more adequate to cope with the problems of his condition now than it was two thousand years ago. The message of Jesus is relevant precisely because it provides the underpinnings of conviction about the basic nature of reality without which we will never be able to change the world. The world is still pretty much the place it was when Jesus came; the reason why is that so few people have thought to take Jesus seriously.

But why is one's fundamental world view so important? Why does it really matter what one thinks about the nature and destiny of the universe? Isn't it enough that we agree with other people on proximate ends without having to share ultimate values with them? These questions, frequently and mindlessly asked, miss the point entirely. Of course we can work with those who share proximate ends with us. The relevant question is not who we can work with but rather what contribution our world view has to make.

There is no room for discouragement. We have the Great Assurance that love will triumph, that it will be all right in the end. Such a conviction does not make things easier. Our bright hopes are frustrated; our dreams blighted. Faith is not an inexpensive tranquilizer that eliminates the need for suffering. All it does—and this of course is critical—is enable us to keep going.

As I write these words the college campuses of the country are quiet. The students with whom I have talked assure me that they and their contemporaries have given up on political action. As one young man expressed it, "We got all excited last spring and didn't accomplish anything, so now we've decided there's not much point in trying." Oh, man of little faith. One effort, without careful analysis or hard work, leading to an emotional outburst and it becomes permissible to be disillusioned. The young people did not take to the streets to support peace candidates in the 1970 election, and Ralph Nader says they have copped out on the ecology-pollution issue. The present generation of enthusiasts have set an all-time record for shortness of commitment.

Their discouragement has only just begun, as anyone who has tried ever so slightly to modify the human condition can tell them. Frustration, discouragement, defeat, and disappointment are constant. If one does not have some fundamental conviction, he will either give up in cynicism or become authoritarian, determined to force men to be virtuous whether they want virtue or not.

Furthermore, in the agonizing complexities and uncertainties of personal relationships, the temptation to quit is overwhelming. Unless one believes that somehow it will be all right, that no matter how much pain and suffering there is in developing an intimate relationship, the struggle is not without purpose.

Discouragement and disappointments, both in social action and human relationships, become even worse as the years advance and one's health and vigor begin to fail. One hoped for so much and so little seems to have occurred. One worked so hard; the payoff was so small. One dreamed such dreams and the reality is so shabby. Maybe Macbeth was right after all; the idiot's tale means nothing. Whether it be the young enthusiast, frustrated because Congress did not change its policy once he has explained his conviction, or the aging reformer who has discovered that even the success of all his plans does not really seem to alter the human condition, discouragement is the ultimate foe; a foe which can be overcome only if one's notion of the fundamental nature of the universe forbids surrender to it.

In G. K. Chesterton's "Ballad of the White Horse," Alfred the Saxon sits disconsolately on an island in the Thames River lamenting the defeat of his armies by the invading Danes. The Mother of God appears to him standing above the reef of the river. He asks her for a sign that his struggle is not in vain. She tells him that a sign he will not get, for while the men in the East may read signs in the stars that give them courage to go on:

> But the men who are signed with the cross of Christ
> Go gaily in the dark.
>
> I tell you not for your comfort,
> Yea, not for your desire
> Save that the sky grows darker yet
> And the sea rises higher.
>
> Night shall be thrice upon you
> And heaven an iron cope
> Do you have joy without a cause
> Or faith without a hope.

"But the men who are signed with the cross of Christ go gaily in the dark": as good a two-line summary of the message of Jesus as one could find. And Alfred the Saxon stands up, buckles on his sword, and goes forth to do battle in the White Horse Vale: as good a Christian response to the message as one could ask for. For Jesus does not say that discouragement will go away; he merely asserts that discouragement is not ultimate. The dark is not any less dark; the gaiety of the Christian is not based on any sign that penetrates that dark, but rather it is a conviction that somewhere ahead there is light which the dark will never extinguish.

A man signed with the cross of Christ can go gaily in the dark precisely because he has the Great Assurance. If one objects that there has been precious little gaiety in the two thousand years of Christian history, the only possible response is that there has been precious little confidence in the Great Assurance. But if gaiety is relevant to the human condition—and I suspect that nothing is more relevant—then the Great Assurance and the Good News of the kingdom are too, so frighteningly relevant in fact that most men will do their best to pretend that neither exists.

He who believes in the kingdom has no choice but to respect and reverence fellow citizens of the kingdom. No cause, however important, justifies his turning his fellow citizens into objects. If God is generous in forgiving, so, certainly, must be His followers. White racists, ethnic hardhats, reactionaries, or, on the other hand, radicals, Communists, and hippies must all be treated with sympathy and respect. No cause, however sacred or just, can legitimate hatred; and no oppressed people, no matter how virtuous, have any right to denounce other people as a class. The long years of discrimination and bigotry, of white against black, do not legitimate black hatred or stereotyping of white. Hatred, stereotyping, bigotry, prejudice of whatever sort have place only in a cynical universe; they are irrelevant in a world in which madly generous Love is defined as the core of reality.

One must be stubborn about the point: the message of Jesus of Nazareth is absolutely meaningless unless it produces men and women who can go gaily in the dark without the need for enemies to scapegoat. There is no way to prove as yet that gaiety and generosity can indeed reform the world, but it's worth nothing that their opposites, cynicism and scapegoating, have not succeeded.

The late George Orwell once remarked that all revolutions fail. But not all the failures are the same. Some revolutions, one presumes, fail because they are beaten and others fail because they succeed. The message of Jesus of Nazareth suggests that attempts to change the world fail because, in the final analysis, men lose their nerve and their confidence. They lose their nerve and their confidence because they do not believe in the kingdom of his Father, a kingdom of love and generosity. Christianity denies no human aspiration; it rather asserts confidently that these aspirations are valid. But its very confidence modifies the style of our pursuit of our aspirations in such a way that now, for the first time, achieving them ought to become possible. To believe it of course takes a tremendous amount of trust in the fundamental goodness of Reality and a good deal of faith in the message which asserts such goodness. If the kingdom of God is at hand and it is moving toward victory with the inevitability of the seed growing into the tree, then we need never lose our cool. For in the long run nothing, not even death, can hurt us. But the people who have kept their cool in the last two thousand years have been few and far between. It is, after all, hard to be cool when one's principal concern is those cotton-pickin' Romans.

By no means does self-definition as Christian guarantee that a person really believes in the kingdom, really accepts the Great Assurance, or really is capable of going gaily in the dark. At some point in the distant past, a decision was made that in the absence of internal acceptance of the Good News, then external conformity to it would suffice. It was much easier, of course, to arrange for external conformity because it is much easier to pretend to be a Christian than to really be one. One's attempts at gaiety may be halfhearted, one's celebrations may be lackadaisical, one's confidence in the Great Assurance may be cautiously guarded, but one can still go through the motions. The training in Catholic schools, seminaries, and novitiates was carefully arranged so that going through the external motions could almost be guaranteed. One's commitment might be rather weak, but the external supports propping up the commitment were quite powerful.

But since the Vatican Council, this strategy has collapsed. We find considerable numbers of priests, religious, and laity who have discovered that their commitment to the kingdom is weak, if it exists at all. One, for example, hears women religious in their middle thirties say that they're not sure their religious order will survive, they're not sure that there will be anyone to take care of them in their old age, that therefore it is necessary for them to leave the community and find an occupation and, eventually, a husband in order that they might have some security. Go gaily in the dark, indeed! Similarly, we hear from priests that they're not sure what the priesthood means anymore, and they do not know whether the Church has a future. But this is simply another way of saying that they never did know what the priesthood meant and they never did know what the Church meant, and they never did commit themselves to the good news of the kingdom. Their lives are not lives of joy and wonder and surprise now because they never were, but in the absence of external support, the weakness of their faith and commitment becomes all too obvious. And Catholic laity are profoundly shocked either by the dramatic changes in the Church or, alternately, with the failure of the Church to change enough. But if their commitment to the kingdom, their belief in the Great Assurance, if their gaiety in the dark depends upon the structures of the organized Church, then it never was much in the way of faith to begin with. It is not that any of these three groups have suddenly lost their cool; rather, they never had the cool in the first place and the collapse of the structures of external conformity simply makes the deficiency obvious. They may try to persuade us that they don't know whether they believe anymore, but the point is that they never really believed at all. But then, very few of us have.

The message of the kingdom is an absurd one. Prudent, careful, cautious, and cynical men will never accept it. They will ask irrelevant questions or pretend to believe the message and then live without confidence and gaiety. I suppose that Jesus was not surprised. He surely understood that the last thing in the world men wanted to hear was good news.

CHAPTER 4

THE CALL FOR A DECISION

In the last century repeated efforts have been made to characterize Jesus as an "ethical teacher." For some men, like A. Loisy and A. Schweitzer, the ethics were essentially gentle and peaceful. More recently some theologians have tried to characterize Jesus' ethical system as revolutionary; many see it as ethics of *political* revolution. But these attempts to find behavioral formulas to specify a response to Jesus are not new. In the very early Church there was a dispute as to whether response to Jesus required obedience to the Mosaic law. In later years those who were most enthusiastic in their response were expected to demonstrate that enthusiasm by venturing forth into the desert or hieing themselves to monasteries where rigidly prescribed rules of conduct were thought to represent the best way of achieving perfection in one's response to Jesus. The religious life as it came into the twentieth century was firmly committed to the notion that, if one followed certain prescriptions and, of course, in every respect the will of one's superior, then one could be confident of the worth of one's response to Jesus. Most recently, some of those on the margins of Christian existentialism see response to Jesus in "personality fulfillment," and in some cases even as "fulfillment" is achieved in sensitivity and encounter groups.

There is a good deal to be said for the religious life

and for personality fulfillment, though endorsing both does not endorse the bizarre aberrations of "pop psychology" or some of the monastic practices such as the penitential disciplines of sixth-century Ireland. In those cases one can be sure that some kind of mental disturbance, sometimes of an extreme variety, has intervened between the message of Jesus and response to it.

But neither can the genius of the religious life nor the quest for personal fulfillment be reduced to formulas; and, a fortiori, the response to Jesus is not subject to description in terms of ethical formula. Indeed, it does prescribe an ethic, not as a way to enter the kingdom, but as a result of an acceptance of the Kingdom. One did not earn admission to the kingdom by being virtuous; the kingdom was a pure gift. Once one had accepted the gift, then there are certain inevitable consequences for an ethical life. Norman Perrin summarizes this insight very nicely:

> In speaking in the way of recognition and response, we are intending to cover ground that might be considered under such a rubric as 'ethics'. But 'ethics' is a misleading word, because it carries with it the assumption that there is a Christian ethic as there is a Socratic or humanistic ethic. So far as the teaching of Jesus is concerned, this latter is simply not true. There is nothing in that teaching about standards of conduct or moral judgements, there is only the urgent call to recognize the challenge of the proclamation and to respond to it. To talk about the "ethical teaching of Jesus" is to talk about something that can only be found by a process of abstraction and deduction from the teaching as a whole. While we may sometimes wish to carry out such a process, let us recognize that it is always a process which does violence, to a greater or lesser degree, to the intent of the historical Jesus.[1]

[1] Norman Perrin, *Rediscovering the Teaching of Jesus.* New York: Harper & Row, 1967, p. 109.

Jesus came to preach good news: the kingdom of his Father was at hand. The fundamental ethical challenge was to accept the kingdom, to choose decisively in favor of it, to become a part of it *now* before it is too late. The splendid, glorious opportunity is at hand, and Jesus pleads with us not to miss it.

The parable of the Ten Virgins has this theme precisely. A great feast is being prepared; the Lord, our God, has come to begin his reign, and the banquet will celebrate that feast. We have a choice of entering into this splendid, joyous celebration or standing aside from it. We are urged to decide which we will do, and we are warned of the fate of those who, like the foolish virgins, procrastinate. If we put off choosing for the kingdom of Jesus' Father, we may find that the opportunity has passed us by.

The same theme is to be found in the parable of the Last Supper, where, according to the Scripture scholars, in Jesus' orginal version the emphasis was not so much on those who were called from the highways and the byways but on those foolish people who refused the invitation to the brilliant and exciting festival. In Jeremias' words:

> This parable, too, is not fully understood until attention is paid to the note of joy which rings through the summons: "everything is ready (v. 17). "Behold, now is the accepted time; behold, now is the day of salvation" [II Cor.6.2]. God fulfils his promises and comes forward out of his hiddenness. But if the "children of the kingdom", the theologians and the pious circles, pay no heed to his call, the despised and ungodly will take their place; the others will receive nothing but a "Too late" from behind the closed doors of the banquet hall.[2]

[2] Joachim Jeremias, *The Parables of Jesus,* Revised Edition. New York: Charles Scribner's Sons, 1963, p. 180.

Jesus pleaded repeatedly with his audiences to respond; indeed, many scholars regard the parables of Jesus as essentially a weapon he used in controversy to demand a response from the listening crowds.

The story of the Unjust Steward (Luke 16: 1–9), which has scandalized so many pious Christians, has but one single point—we must act decisively while there is still time. Norman Perrin translates the parable into a modern idiom.

'There was a certain labour racketeer who had grown rich on sweetheart contracts and illegal use of the union pension fund. One day he found that the FBI was tailing him and he began to suspect that there was no escape for him. So what did he do? Carefully, he put a large sum of money away where no one could touch it and then faced trial. He was duly convicted and after he had exhausted all his rights to appeal, he finally served a sentence in the Atlanta Federal penitentiary. Having served his time, he took his money and moved to Miami Beach, where he lived happily ever after.'[3]

The steward (labor racketeer) was scarcely an admirable person, but at least he was capable of decision. When he was in a difficult situation, with time running out, he acted decisively. He saw a crisis which threatened him with ruin and disaster, and he did not let things overwhelm him; he acted. And while he acted dishonestly, he did act. So, we too are faced with disaster if we pass up the invitation to become part of the kingdom. Like the unjust steward we must act boldly, resolutely, and courageously, for if we do not, we will have suffered a tragic loss.

Similarly, Jesus urges us to keep our hand on the plow and not look back. His audiences of course knew what

[3] Perrin, *op. cit.*, p. 115.

he meant; the Palestinian plow was a light wooden implement, and if someone looked away from the furrow he was digging, it could easily swerve to one side and the furrow would become crooked. There is not time for us to look back; we must move ahead decisively. If we hesitate and look back, the furrows of our lives will become crooked and we may steer ourselves outside the kingdom.

Jesus' famous saying about the need to hate one's family if one wishes to be worthy of him (a saying of such scandalous vigor that the critics are agreed that it must have come from him) is another way of trying to create a sense of urgency in his audience. The matter at hand is of such grave consequence that even one's family must not be permitted to interfere with his making the decisive choice in favor of the kingdom of the Father.

The ethics of the kingdom, then, are a consequence of the choice that one makes. Perrin points out to us that even the parable of the Good Samaritan, which is surely an ethical parable par excellence, is a parable rooted in Jesus' eschatological message of the kingdom of the Father.

> Because one knows God as responding to human needs in terms of the eschatological forgiveness of sins, one must respond to the needs of a neighbour in terms of whatever may be appropriate to the immediate situation.[4]

The Jew and the Samaritan were bitter enemies, but because God had expended loving forgiveness to the Samaritan, he in turn extends love to the Jew he finds in need. As Perrin puts it, "In the context of God's forgiveness men learn to forgive, and in the exercise of forgiveness toward their fellow man they enter ever more deeply into an experience of the divine forgiveness.[5] Or, in other

[4] Perrin, *op. cit.*, p. 124.
[5] *Ibid.*, p. 152.

words, as men experience God's love for them, they respond to other human beings with love and, in that response, come to understand God's love better.

The behavior of the Christian, then, is indeed the behavior of a man transformed, a man who has undergone
a *metanoia*. But repentance is not accomplished the way
one acquires skills at water skiing, knitting, or writing books.
It is rather a transformation of one's life that is accomplished in a basic existential leap in which we decisively
choose for the kingdom of God, decisively commit ourselves
to the notion that the Really Real is in fact insanely generous love. The ethical behavior of the Christian is a consequence of that leap, not an automatic consequence, indeed,
because the leap is never perfect or complete; not a consequence which requires little effort, but a consequence that
follows inevitably just the same. For if we permit ourselves
to experience God's love, then that love is so powerful that
it bursts forth from our personality and spreads to all around
us. The light breaks forth in the darkness, and the darkness cannot put it out.

So much of the approach to Christian ethics in ages
past has been the other way around. Whatever the theological differences have been, and whatever the theoretical
debates, in fact most of us have preferred to believe that
our ethics earn us admission to the kingdom. During the
Reformation, for example, both the reformers and the
fathers of the Council of Trent agreed that one could not
merit on one's own the initial admission to the kingdom.
But in fact, Protestants and Catholics alike since the six-
teenth century have lived their lives as though Christianity
was an exercise of certain carefully detailed specific responsibilities. The New Testament provides no grounds for
such an assumption; on the contrary, Jesus makes it clear
that the essential challenge is to accept the kingdom. That
is the major ethical act. When that is accomplished all
else follows "naturally," even if not without pain and dif-

ficulty. Jesus resisted attempts to categorize the behavior of those who accepted the Father's kingdom in terms of specific regulations. The parable of the Good Samaritan was the response to just such a question which sought for a neat juridical definition of what a neighbor is. Rather, the emphasis in Jesus' teaching was on concrete situations and concrete responses to the situations. Norman Perrin, in discussing the concept of faith as described in the miracle stories (and he does not doubt, by the way, that there is a hard core of authenticity in the miracle stories), writes:

> Today, the pupils of the original form critics are prepared to accept elements of the tradition their teachers rejected. We cannot, of course, diagnose the diseases and their cures over the gulf of two thousand years and radically different Weltanschauungen. Nor can we accept the necessary authenticity of any single story as it stands at present in the synoptic tradition; the "legendary overlay" (Kasemann) and the influence of parallel stories from Hellenism and Judaism on the tradition are too strong for that. But we can say that behind that tradition there must lie a hard core of authenticity. . . .[6]

Faith in a concrete situation, faith in Jesus' demands of his followers, is not acceptance of some abstract, theoretical proposition, but rather the commitment of the total person, the concrete situation presented by God's intervention in history in the form of the kingdom proclaimed by Jesus.

I am not suggesting, of course, that there is no room for theory in Christianity, no room for abstract propositions, no room for philosophical systems. Man must reflect and he must especially reflect on those central symbols around which he organizes the whole meaning system of his life. But the symbols precede analysis; they do not follow it.

[6] *Ibid.*, p. 136.

The full understanding of the implications of our decision to accept the kingdom of Jesus' Father goes not before we have committed ourselves to the kingdom but after. The whole history of Christianity is the history of people claiming to have responded to Jesus' urgent demand for decision, while in fact they have not responded to it, of people proclaiming that they believe all the truths of the faith but of hesitating to commit the whole reality of what they are to the fundamental truths of the insanely generous love of God for us.

Jesus made the issue very simple and pleaded with us to make up our minds, and we have responded by making the issue very complex. We pretend that we have made up our minds and try to live in the world between commitment and noncommitment, between apathy and joy, between going to the wedding banquet and staying away, between seizing the opportunity of the moment and decisively rejecting that opportunity. Like the ten foolish virgins, we sit at the door of the feast and proclaim that in just a minute we are going to go in, but never quite get around to walking over the threshold.

If one views the story of Christianity as a long chronicle of how people have evaded the decision that Jesus expects of them, a lot of puzzles are solved, but one still must ask, why? Why are we so afraid to respond to Jesus' urgent demand for an answer?

I once had an opportunity to work with a small group of people who in their history together seem to have recapitulated the whole story of Christianity. They discovered almost by chance that there was a possibility of leading a different kind of life, a life of hope and love and joy, of giving themselves over to commitment to the kingdom which Jesus had come to preach. But, then, suddenly they realized the immense demands that the commitment would make on them for the rest of their lives, how much they would have to give up, how many of their foolish fears and defenses they would have to put away, how open their lives would be to ridicule and laughter, the many risks they would have to take. It was not at all clear that the joy and love were worth the price that had to be paid. Rather than take the chance, the group, both as individuals and as a collectivity, fell back on the defensive patterns of their childhood. Some became silent, some became aggressive, some became manipulative, some became disruptive. It was decided that they were not a religious group but merely a friendship community. God, Jesus, Christianity, the kingdom were mentioned only at the risk of exposing oneself to sarcastic laughter. It was argued that all of us must accept everyone the way they were, that no demands, no challenges, no insistence on *metanoia* were acceptable. Ours was a friendship community and friendship meant "total acceptance." Those who tried to preach and practice something else were driven forth, and though the original group soon lost all vitality and direction, and indeed practically all trust and affection, it still persists, if only so as to assure the remnants of its membership not merely that no negative decision was made, but also that no response had ever been required.

The most appalling part of the story is not the rejection of the kingdom which was inherent in this group's history —and I am completely persuaded that the group did indeed reject Jesus and his message—but the dishonesty of the refusal even to acknowledge that Jesus was rejected. One can imagine the Lord saying, "Why won't you at least say no to me, if you will not say yes? Why do you persist either in pretending that there is no need to say yes or no, or in pretending that you have already said yes when, in fact, you live as though you had said no?"

But this little band of people was no different from those who listened to Jesus in Palestine two thousand years ago, and most of those who have claimed to follow him ever since. People do not want to let go. If Jesus will let them

reduce his message to certain formulary that can be scru-
pulously carried out, fine. If one can obey canon law or be
"totally open and honest" in an encounter group, if one
honors all the precise regulations of the constitutions in one's
community, if one zealously pursues the radical party line
on every moral issue that occurs, then one is only too willing
to be a follower of Jesus, because in all these responses one
is still in control. One's own selfhood is still nicely contained. The force of God's love is carefully limited. The
stirrings of the spirit are neatly arranged. The precise timetable has been prepared for the coming of the kingdom.
But the response that Jesus demands, the existential leap
of being in the world, this we would rather not do because
we would not be able to control ourselves or contain the
power of the spirit or the fierceness of God's love.

The only difference between the little community of
which I have spoken and its predecessors in the long and
sorry history of Christian refusal to respond to Jesus is that
this community was sophisticated in matters psychological.
It not only used childish defense mechanisms to keep God
and one another at bay, but it became quite self-conscious
about these mechanisms and tried to persuade itself that its
real problem was not the absence of religious commitment
but rather the presence of interpersonal difficulties. That
psychological stresses and strains were there was surely true
—they are present in every human relationship. What was
also true was that these strains were jealously guarded and
eagerly promoted because as long as one could concentrate
on interpersonal hangups there was no need to address
oneself to the ever-present but conveniently obscured challenge of Jesus.

In the forties and fifties (and for centuries before, for
that matter) there was little awareness of the connection
between religious commitment and personality growth; in

the last decade, the pendulum has swung in the opposite direction and the two have been equated. Psychological categories are extremely helpful in helping us to understand the nature of man's religious problem, but it is of utmost importance that one think clearly about the relationship between faith and personality.

In their very root, one supposes they are the same, for acceptance of the kingdom and acceptance of life in all its fullness are virtually the same act. Anyone who responds positively to the invitation to the wedding feast has opened himself up to the world and to his fellow man in hope, love, and joy and is on his way to human wholeness. The reason for this is that the Good News asserts that man's hunger for the absolute and the ultimate, for life and love, is a valid hunger and one to which Life and Love will respond. The message of the kingdom asserts that the fundamental thrust of the human personality is in fact a response to the Really Real.

Thus, religious growth and personality development go hand in hand. The fundamental difference that the Christian message makes is simply that it provides greater assurance and deeper confidence that the thrust is not a vain one. One can develop and enrich one's personality without accepting explicitly and consciously the Christian message. In every thrust of the human person to transcend the limitations of his being, there is certainly an implicit, at least at the time of commitment, notion that reality is good. What Christianity adds is a great deal more confidence and assurance that the struggle for wholeness is worth the price and that it will ultimately end in triumph. The difference between the Christian seeking to become fully himself and the non-Christian may simply be the difference between explicit and confident acceptance of the Good News and an implicit and tentative acceptance of it. But that is the whole purpose of Jesus' coming with his message: to make explicit and conscious that which previously had been implicit and very tentative.

The consequence of this line of reasoning is that when someone is explicitly faced with the message of Jesus and understands what that message is, a response which says, "I will proceed to develop my personality" is something less than an adequate response, because Jesus' challenge, at least to those who hear and understand, is a challenge for explicit, conscious, confident and permanent response. He who understands this challenge and tries to limit his response to an implicit affirmation is caught in a difficult if not impossible psychological bind. He says in effect, "I am not ready to commit myself totally to the proposition that the Really Real is insanely generous Love, but I am going to try to become a fuller human being, although I hesitate to make such a commitment and may refuse to do so." This is, of course, a response which declares that life is indeed a tale told by an idiot. He is really saying, "I will live my life in such a way that, if nothingness is my reward, it will be an unjust treatment of me and my life."

In any case, it must be clearly established that Jesus demanded far more in the way of response than that of the atheist or agnostic existentialist who says, "I will become more fully human despite the fact that I think life is absurd," or of the modern Christian who says, "I will become more fully human without addressing myself positively or negatively to the invitation of Jesus." For that invitation is a highly concrete invitation with a highly concrete promise. Jesus demands that we accept his Good News that reality is love and that we open ourselves up so that love flows into us and out of us to all around. The enthusiastic acceptance of the invitation to the wedding feast involved in this challenge may not be the only way to become more fully human, but one is forced to assert that it is the best way that man has yet devised.

Almost at once the question arises, "Why are there so few

Christians who are the kind of loving, living, rejoicing human beings that response to the message of Jesus seems to imply?" The answer to that question is that when a Christian is defined as one who explicitly and consciously says yes to the invitation of Jesus, there are not very many Christians and never have been.

Personal transformation, then, of the gospel message comes about not from engaging in certain ethical acts but from a total transformation of one's life from unbelief to belief. Try as we might to cloud the issue, Jesus will have none of our evasions. He who is not with me is against me. He who does not gather with me scatters. Either the absurd message of joy that Jesus brings ought to be rejected out of hand as blithering idiocy or it must be accepted and lived by. The solution most of us Christians arrive at is to accept it and live by it just enough to get by, just enough to be able to say to Jesus, "At least we are not against you. We can't be with you enough to really enjoy the wedding feast, to become fully and richly ourselves at the feast, and we probably won't be gay and joyful enough to attract others in, but here we are anyway." In other words, we say to Jesus, "Okay, we'll go up on the mountaintop and light a candle— I hope nobody gets a good look at our light."

Let there be no mistake about it: indecisiveness is ultimately a rejection of the message of Jesus, and there is much in the history of the Church that represents rejection. Triumphalism, which puts confidence in the power and the splendor of the Church rather than in the power and love of God, is a rejection. Parochialism, which is too willing to prevent the Father from working outside the Church or the Spirit from inspiring those who are not Catholic, is a rejection. Dishonesty, which tries to obscure the all too obvious human failings in the Church organization, is a rejection of the message of Jesus. The validity of that message does not depend on the virtue of those who preside over that community which is attempting to respond to it. One of the worst of all forms of rejection is authoritarianism, which attempts to compel people to be virtuous. Jesus made it very clear that we had to choose and that the choice must be a completely free one. He compelled no one to follow him, and when the Church uses coercion to win followers for Jesus, it utterly perverts his style and message. Stereotyping and scapegoating, which blame other people for what is wrong in the world, is an utter perversion of the message. When old blames young and young blames old, when white blames black and black blames white, when Catholic blames Protestant and Protestant blames Catholic, each refuses to look into his own heart to see how he has failed to respond. But then it's always so much easier to analyze somebody else's failures instead of our own.

But if the Church frequently fails as a collectivity to decide for or against Jesus, so too do individuals. Pietism is a failure because it confuses commitment with performing certain virtuous acts or developing certain virtuous styles. Zealotry is a failure because it makes us think we can demonstrate our commitment by forcing a commitment on others. Rationalism is a failure because it ultimately refuses to admit the possibility of a special intervention of the Real in the person of Jesus. And faddism is a failure because it confuses being up to date and being "with it" with penetrating the root questions which all men must ask and for which Jesus claimed to have a spectacular answer.

Is there then a crisis of faith in our times? Perhaps there is, but then there always has been a crisis in faith. The difference in our time is merely that many people who have thought that one or more of the evasions mentioned above were in fact faith have now suddenly discovered that these evasions are not indeed adequate answers to the challenge of Jesus, and that he is still insistently urging us to make up our minds whether we want to come to the wedding feast or not. Some of us who always thought that we had accepted the invitation are now discovering that in fact we had not.

The masks and props which have supported us have been taken away and we find ourselves faced with the necessity of deciding whether there is indeed a wedding feast and whether we want to go to it. We hesitate at the doorway. There is music and love and laughter within but maybe it's all a trick. Besides, how many of our problems can be blamed on the people who have organized the feast, and what is the position of those inside on race or on peace or on pollution? They keep saying that if we come into the feast everything will be all right in the end, that black and white will come to love one another, that men can live in peace with each other, and that the world, groaning for redemption, will be redeemed. That's all well and good, we say in response, but would they please give us some sign, and in the meantime, what are they going to do about the Establishment or the military-industrial complex, or about the war? and they answer, "Seek first the wedding feast and all else will be taken care of." Still we hesitate. At one time we thought we were at the feast, but we discover that the banquet that we were attending was only a pale imitation— a counterfeit. Maybe this new wedding feast will be a fake too. We are angry at what happened before. Why should we choose again? After all, what do we owe those people in there at the banquet? What do we owe the one who has convened it? While we hesitate in the doorway, a man comes to the entrance, looks us directly in the eye, and says, "You'd better come in before it's too late. My Father isn't going to keep the door open forever." We know who this man is. He has been preaching this message of urgency for a long time, so we don't feel obliged to take him too seriously. In fact, nobody has ever taken him very seriously.

CHAPTER 5

"WHO DID HE THINK HE WAS?"

In the Irish community I know best the question, "Who does he think he is?" (or if directed to the person, "Who do you think you are?") is the most devastating and sarcastic of conversational ploys. It may be a relic of the poverty of the old country in which virtually all Irishmen shared. When anyone dared to raise himself up as being just a little bit better off than his neighbor, it was felt that he really had no right to do so; that by becoming a little bit affluent he betrayed the cause of Ireland by selling out to the Anglo-Irish Establishment. "Who do you think you are?" is not just a challenge to an upstart but a charge of treason. It was in something of the same sense, one suspects, that Jesus was challenged to explain who he was. Not merely was he a relatively uneducated Galilean peasant, he was also preaching a doctrine which could easily affect the future of the battered Jewish nation. He had better explain himself and explain himself clearly. Who, after all, did he think he was?

Jesus gave a very clear answer, so clear that there ought not to have been any doubt, and yet down through the centuries people have come up with interpretations which would explain away the answer. They are still busy doing so.

One troubled priest observed to me, "But what if Jesus

really didn't claim to be the Messiah after all?" I must say
that whenever I hear a question like that I find it hard to
suppress my amusement. It is as though we are imposing
on Jesus the requirement that he speak in exactly those
categories that would enable him to fit smoothly and pain-
lessly into the categories of Apologetics 101. In other words,
why wasn't Jesus considerate enough to provide ready-made
answers for the questions which we happen to think are
pertinent today? Why did he not give us nice neat dis-
courses on the Trinity, the Incarnation, infallibility of the
pope, collegiality of the bishops, and all the other important
theological questions? It would make things a lot easier for
all of us, or so we like to think.

But did Jesus really think he was the Messiah? The first
thing that must be said is that he apparently was extremely
reluctant to apply titles to himself, in part because titles
represented religious themes that he could not accept. Thus,
the Messiah was thought of as a Davidic political king, and
Jesus did not only not claim political kingship but explicitly
rejected it. Whether he described himself as "the servant
of the Lord" or "son of man" is debated by the contemporary scholars. To put the matter more precisely, by the
strict canons of their science Scripture scholars cannot exclude the possibility that those two titles were not attached
to Jesus by the early Church, so they cannot say that the
use of them was a part of the message of the historical
Jesus.

Most writers would agree that the combination of the son
of man and the suffering servant in St. Mark's gospel and
their application to him by the early Church were perfectly
legitimate conclusions from what we know to be Jesus' authentic message, whether he used them himself or not. It
must be kept in mind that Jesus was not preaching himself.
He was proclaiming the Good News of his Father's kingdom.
Nor was he (despite many decades of writing in this cen-

tury to the contrary) primarily concerned with some future event. He was proclaiming the kingdom of God as present *now* and demanding a response to that kingdom—even though he knew that the kingdom was not yet fully present.

However, after Easter, there was an inevitable shift in emphasis and Jesus the Proclaimer became also the one who was proclaimed. While Jesus was still among them his followers were constrained to concentrate on the message that he preached. But when he had departed and they had their overwhelming experience of him as alive after his death and burial, they had to explain not only the proclamation but the one who proclaimed it. They fell back on the categories they had at hand, the Christ, Son of Man, Servant of God, the Prophet, though obviously they used these categories in a somewhat different fashion than they were used in other contemporary religious thinking. What the early Christians did was what any man must do: they took the symbols available to them and tried to use them to convey the reality of their experience.

At one stage in New Testament criticism, it was at least implied that this early Christian theological thinking about Jesus was consciously or unconsciously a plot in which the basic message of the person of Jesus was distorted. More recent scholarship, however, emphasizes that the experience of Jesus was too powerful for anyone to dare to try to change it. The tradition recounting his life was too sacred to be treated with anything but the utmost respect. What the early Christians, preachers and then writers, attempted was to use symbols to convey and in part to explain their experience of Jesus. The symbols they used were the best ones they could find to relate honestly what they had seen and heard and felt. Furthermore, contemporary writers like Reginald H. Fuller[1] emphasize that according to what we now know about the historical message of Jesus, the sym-

---

[1] Reginald H. Fuller, *The Foundations of New Testament Christology.* New York: Charles Scribner's Sons, 1965.

bols the early Christians chose to use were quite appropriate. What the scholars still disagree on is whether the servant and the son of man symbols were also used in some fashion by Jesus himself. Nevertheless, the use of them by his followers was true to the reality he represented.

Fuller goes even further. He demonstrates at great length and in considerable subtle detail how the theology of the Church as contained even in the first Council is consistent with the intuition of those who wrote the New Testament as well as with the experience of those who knew Jesus. In Fuller's words, ". . . in Jesus Christ an event occurred which transcended all human possibilities. The transcendent salvation became completely immanent in him."[2] He goes on to say:

> And we shall, it is to be hoped, continually return to the ontic mythology when we sing in our Christmas carols:
>
> > Sacred infant, all divine,
> > What a tender love was thine,
> > Thus to come from highest bliss,
> > Down to such a world as this.
>
> And we shall continue to mark with reverence the words of the Nicene Creed, "And was incarnate by the Holy Ghost of the Virgin Mary, and was made man." For although both carol and creed are couched in mythological language, they are the very life-blood of Christian faith and truth, which asserts that Jesus Christ is the saving act of God.[3]

Fuller's account of the development from the experience Jesus' followers had of him through the first primitive theology of the categories used in the New Testament to the

[2] *Ibid.*, p. 256.
[3] *Ibid.*, p. 256.

far more elaborate theologizing necessitated by contact with
the Greek world and culminating in the work of the early
councils may be profoundly shocking to those Christians
who think that it is necessary for Jesus to have thought of
himself in exactly those categories used by the Councils
of Ephesus and Chalcedon. But if we reflect for just a
moment we will see how absurd such an assumption is.
From the point of view of the social scientist, I must say
that Fuller's account makes a great deal of sense. First of
all, man experiences God profoundly, powerfully, as being
present in a very special way. In trying to describe this
experience to others, he uses, modifies, and adjusts the
religious symbols available to him. Then as he moves into
other cultures, he tries to integrate into his presentation
philosophical symbols. Finally, when the community of
those committed to that experience becomes organized, he
strives to elaborate a precise theological synthesis, hoping, of
course, that the clarity and precision of the synthesis does no
serious harm to the vitality and energy of the original insight and experience. It does seem to me that anyone who
is committed to the notion of Chalcedon, that Jesus was
truly man, will not be shocked that his followers understood
him and expressed that understanding in a truly human
way.

So whether Jesus called himself the Christ or not (and
he probably did not) is a rather irrelevant question. What
is relevant is whether the early Christian use of this word
regarding him was true to his message. And whether he
called himself or thought of himself as the Son of Man
or the Suffering Servant (and he may have) is of less
importance than whether the use of these symbols does
convey to us something very important about who Jesus
was and what his message was. The work of men like Fuller
and A. J. B. Higgins[4] makes, it seems to me, an entirely

[4] A. J. B. Higgins, *Jesus and the Son of Man*. Philadelphia: Fortress
Press, 1964.

persuasive case that the use of these symbols was perfectly valid.

But then how did Jesus think of himself? To answer this question, we must turn more to his words and deeds than to any titles that he appropriated for himself. Jesus claimed that in his words the kingdom of God is really present. In the solemn introduction, "Truly, I say to you," by this "'Amen', Jesus pledges," Fuller says, "his whole person behind the truth of his proclamation."[5] In the message of Jesus, in other words, one is confronted with the actual presence of the kingdom of God not only in his words but in his deeds also.

Jesus claims that God is present by acting through him. As Fuller puts it, "It is demonstrated by logia which pass all the criteria of authenticity."[6] Jesus addresses people with the phrase, "Truly I say to you." He is not interpreting or reporting a tradition like the rabbis do. Nor is he relating a message received from a distant God like the Old Testament prophets did. God is not distant at all; he is near enough to be called by the intimate title, "Abba." In Fuller's words:

> The nearness of God is *now* a reality precisely in his drawing near in Jesus' eschatological ministry, which is therefore implicitly christological. Jesus can call God "Abba" because he has known him as the one who has drawn nigh in his own word and deed . . .[7]

All of Jesus' behavior—his announcing of the kingdom, his call for decision, his demand for a response, his teaching about the nearness of God, his urging others to follow

[5] Fuller, *op. cit.*, p. 104.
[6] *Ibid.*, p. 105.
[7] *Ibid.*, p. 106.

him, his eating with publicans and sinners—"forces upon us the conclusion that underlying his word and work is an implicit Christology. In Jesus as he understood himself, there is an immediate confrontation with 'God's presence and his very self' offering judgment and salvation."[8]

Fuller concludes his argument by asserting:

> . . . he was certainly conscious of a unique Sonship to which he was privileged to admit others through his es-chatological ministry. For, although there is no indubitably authentic legion in which Jesus calls himself the "Son", he certainly called God his Father in a unique sense.[9]

In other words, Jesus thought of himself, preached, and behaved as though he was the Son of God in a special and unique sense. This was how his followers perceived him, this was the message they conveyed in the New Testament, and this is the experience and the message which the formularies of Chalcedon and Ephesus tried to reduce to theological precision.

In a way, that's all that really matters. Jesus is the Son of God, God is uniquely present in him, both in his words and his deeds; and when we experience Jesus we experience contact with the Father who is present in him. What he chose to call himself on different occasions is quite irrelevant compared to the overwhelming import of his words and deeds.

But one would have thought that it was obvious. A. J. B. Higgins, speaking of both the Son of God and the Son of Man and their Christologies, observes: "The genesis of both Christologies, however, is undoubtedly to be found in the thought of Jesus, only the result is further from that thought in the case of the latter than in that of the former,

8 *Ibid.*, p. 106.
9 *Ibid.*, p. 115.

for Jesus certainly believed God to be his Father in a
unique and special sense."[10] He concludes his book with
the observation:

> Jesus' fundamental understanding of his mission thus went
> far beyond . . . the thought of the humiliation and exalta-
> tion of the righteous in contemporary Judaism. It was
> conditioned by a much more profound consideration—the
> consciousness of his sonship to the Father, Abba.[11]

Fuller and Higgins both state it nicely. (British Scripture
scholars writing in the Anglican tradition have a much
more graceful way of expressing themselves than those
who write in the German Lutheran tradition.) But how
could there have been any doubt? If one reads the New
Testament to find an absolutely precise justification of the
formulations of Ephesus and Chalcedon, he will be disappointed. If one reads to discover how Jesus thought of
himself, the evidence is overwhelming that he thought of
himself as the Son of God in a special and unique way.
He believed that the Father was closely and intimately
present in him, and that those who followed him followed
the Father also. Jesus was not the pious, ethical teacher;
nor was he the prophet come to announce an immediate
apocalypse. As we shall see in a later chapter, Jesus was
not especially interested in the end of things. He was concerned about the present challenge. The notion that Jesus
was an ethical teacher and apocalyptic prophet is one of
the most extraordinarily clever and systematic conspiracies
that man has ever developed. The New Testament presents
Jesus as claiming something entirely different. He asserted
that in him and through him God was intimately present
in human events, an idea completely foreign if not repug-

[10] Higgins, op. cit., p. 202.
[11] Ibid., p. 208.

nant to all the religious currents of his time (or any other
time, for that matter). He was either what he said or a
madman, and the attempt to write him off as something
else is false both to the New Testament as we have it
now and to his own message revealed by the Scripture
scholars as they probe beyond the words of the New Testament to find the historical Jesus himself.

The German scholar Joachim Jeremias in his pamphlet,
"*The Lord's Prayer*"[12] and his book, *The Central Message
of the New Testament*,[13] makes much of the word *abba*.
Indeed, Jeremias argues that if we only had the two authentic words of Jesus, *amen* and *abba* (and both are indis-
putably authentic), we would have enough to be able
to understand his message. For the word *amen* indicates
he was one who preached on his own authority, and the
word *abba* indicates that he was one who claimed the
most intimate of possible connections with God, his Father.
Jeremias does not feel that he exaggerates a bit when he
says that all we know of both the person and the message
of Jesus can be summarized in those two words.

Jeremias attaches enormous importance to Jesus' use of
the word *abba:* "To date nobody has produced one single
instance in Palestinian Judaism where God is addressed as
'my Father' by an individual person."[14] Furthermore, nowhere in the immense literature of ancient Judaism is there
a single instance of the invocation of God as *Abba*. It is
a word of utmost intimacy and familiarity. It was the
babbling sound that a Jewish infant used toward his
father, the equivalent of "dada." But it was more than that.
Grown-up sons and daughters called their fathers *Abba*
as well, but only in the context of the greatest tenderness
and familiarity. It is never used in Jewish prayers because

[12] Joachim Jeremias, "*The Lord's Prayer*," trans. by John Reumann,
Facet Books Biblical Series—8. Philadelphia: Fortress Press, 1964.
[13] Joachim Jeremias, *The Central Message of the New Testament*. New
York: Charles Scribner's Sons, 1965.
[14] *Ibid.*, Message, p. 16.

"to a Jewish mind," Jeremias says, "it would have been irreverent and therefore unthinkable to call God by this familiar word."[15] For Jesus to dare to use this word, to speak with God as a child speaks with his father, intimately, simply, and securely, is for Jeremias, "something new, something unique, and something unheard of . . ."[16]

Beyond all doubt, *abba* is a word that Jesus did use, and when we have established that he used it:

> We are confronted with something new and unheard of which breaks through the limits of Judaism. Here we see who the historical Jesus was: the man who had the power to address God as *Abba* and who included the sinners and the publicans in the kingdom by authorizing them to repeat this one word, '*Abba,* dear Father'.[17]

For Jeremias, then, the "Our Father" is a prayer of utmost importance. His booklet is extremely interesting reading because it shows the fantastic scholarly care and cleverness by which the Scripture researcher recreates the original Aramaic text of the Lord's Prayer. As Jeremias notes:

> . . . in the Lord's Prayer Jesus authorizes his disciples to repeat the word *abba* after him. He gives them a share in his sonship and empowers them, as his disciples, to speak with the heavenly Father in just such a familiar, trusting way as a child would with his father. Yes, he goes so far as to say that it is this new childlike relationship which first opens the doors to God's reign: "Truly, I say to you, unless you become like children again, you will not find entrance into the kingdom of God" [Matt. 18:3]. Children can say "*abba*"! Only he who, through Jesus, lets

---

[15] *Ibid.*, Message, p. 21.
[16] *Ibid.*, Message, p. 21.
[17] *Ibid.*, Message, p. 30.

himself be given the childlike trust which resides in the word *abba* finds his way into the kingdom of God. This the apostle Paul also understood; he says twice that there is no surer sign or guarantee of the possession of the Holy Spirit and of the gift of sonship than this, that a man makes bold to repeat this one word, *"Abba,* dear Father" [Rom. 8:15; Gal. 4:6]. Perhaps at this point we get some inkling why the use of the Lord's Prayer was not a commonplace in the early church and why it was spoken with such reverence and awe: "Make us worthy, O Lord, that we joyously and without presumption may make bold to invoke Thee, the heavenly God, as Father, and to say, Our Father."[18]

The phrase "we presume to say" or "we dare to say" is very ancient. It goes back into the first century. I suppose that most of us who repeated the words every day at Mass *"audemus dicure"* thought of it as a quaint Latin phrase. We did not realize how bold and daring, how outrageous, how almost blasphemous it was to use such a word of God. Indeed, some of the untrained liturgical enthusiasts quickly dropped the phrase when liturgical reform began. Once again we missed the point completely. Jesus was not merely the one so intimate with the Father that he would dare to address Him in a familiar tone; he was also the one to make it possible for the rest of us to speak to God, the Really Real, the Ground of Being, the Absolute, the Ultimate, the Infinite, in terms of affectionate familiarity. When Jesus called God *"Abba,"* he urged us to do so too; and that is the core of the message he proclaimed. We have called God *"Abba"* down through the centuries, but whether we have actually lived as though we were on such intimate terms with the Really Real is another matter entirely.

Louis Evely, the resigned French priest, has recently

[18] Jeramias, *"The Lord's Prayer,"* op. cit., pp. 20–21.

launched a fierce attack on the "Our Father," suggesting that it inculcates fear, insecurity, dependency, and anxiety. Nowhere in his attack, which in my judgment borders on the blasphemous, is there any awareness of what men like Fuller and Jeremias have come to understand is the implication of the use of the word *abba*. Evely is obviously very angry at what the Church has done to him—so angry that he would sooner attack the "Our Father" than address himself to the challenge and demand for a response that the word *abba* clearly conveys. Evely is not the first man to miss the point; nor is he the last. It is so very easy to be angry at the mistakes of our teachers and leaders. It is so difficult to penetrate beyond our anger to face the horrendous existential challenge implicit in the life of a man who thought himself to be God's son, called God, "Daddy dear," and instructed us to do so too.

In another book, *The Gospels Without Myth*, Evely urges that we strip myth away from the gospel, arguing a popularized and bowdlerized version of R. K. Bultmann. But religious thought without symbols is impossible, and Evely only substitutes his symbols of psychological self-fulfillment for those of ancient Jewish thought, which were, after all, the only ones available to the writers of the New Testament. It would have been much more helpful and more scholarly, too, if Evely had suggested that we strive to understand the fundamental religious experience the New Testament authors were trying to convey through their use of the terms Messiah, Son of Man, and Suffering Servant. That perhaps they struggled to communicate their encounter with the man Jesus, who claimed that the distant God was near—indeed, present—in his word and deed; and that God was not only available to him on terms of affectionate familiarity but also available to us in the same terms so long as we followed him.

One must imagine how profoundly disconcerting Jesus' words and deeds were to his contemporaries. Not only did he refuse to answer what they thought were relevant questions, he refused to put a label on himself that would enable them to pigeonhole him in categories of their own religious thought. More than that, he introduced a completely new set of categories—startling, shocking, blasphemous categories. The way Jesus spoke and acted was unsettling, jarring, troubling. Any man who dared to use such language was bound to cause trouble. The language was so new and startling that it was difficult to say even what the nature of his trouble would be. Finally, the authorities settled on the kind of trouble they thought would be most appealing to the Roman government. The Romans could only have thought anyone using "Daddy dear" to address God was a harmless madman; they had to consider him a potential rebel. So, although Jesus denied that he was a political messiah, he was still executed on that charge. But deep down inside, the real problem was that he made himself like God; he even went so far as to suggest that in his name we could too.

We have incarcerated this claim of Jesus into harmless, trite formulations which, though frequently repeated have no concrete impact on our lives. Theological arguments by angry men like Louis Evely are most welcome because they provide us with an escape from having to face and deal with the apparent blasphemy of Jesus' behavior. It is better to denounce mythology, or to argue about *homoousios* or *homoiousios;* better to repeat mechanically the Our Father a hundred times a day than to permit ourselves to face the historic and terrible reality of Jesus' claim.

Would it not have been wiser for Jesus to compromise just a bit? Even if he did think of himself as being able to say *amen* and *abba,* would it not have been more discreet and prudent to avoid such language? Could he not have conveyed the Good News of God's loving eschatological intervention in history without adding the bizarre claim that that intervention was somehow personified in himself? The message was hard enough to accept. Why create additional scandal by identifying himself with that message? Those who came after him would have to cope with not just the message, not just the absurdity that God is a lover, passionate to the point of insanity, but also with the blasphemy that God becomes intimately available to us in the person of Jesus. Would it not have been more difficult for us to evade the message of Jesus if he had not also included himself as someone, in a way, even more terrifying than the message? Why was he not content with the perfectly exciting Good News that God did love us and was intervening in a merciful and saving way? Why did he have to embellish the Good News with the even more incredible announcement that through him we could address the Ground of Being as Daddy. As we noted in a previous chapter, men don't particularly like those who bring good news, especially when that news is so good as to seem ridiculously absurd. Why did Jesus have to make the Good News so fantastically good? Why did he have to suggest that he was intimately part of the Good News? Could he not have soft-pedaled somewhat the whole *abba*, and *amen* business?

All of which is, of course, another way of wondering if Jesus couldn't have pulled his punches just a bit. We are no longer asking, Who did he think he was? We are now asking, Why did he have to burden us with the knowledge of who he thought he was?

But there is no sign of his willingness to compromise; no indication of his willingness to make concessions to our disinclination to take the risk of believing him. He was a man with serene confidence in the nature of his mission and absolute uncompromising integrity in its execution. He was sorry when people would not believe him, sorry to the point of weeping over the city of Jerusalem, but he neither pleaded nor threatened, neither argued nor cajoled. He was not defensive and did not apologize. He was authentic but not with the phony authenticity that is so popular today—that kind of authenticity that attempts to overwhelm others. He was patient in the face of those who deliberately missed the point. He explained, but it usually made matters worse instead of better. He clarified, but it seemed to confuse his audience even more. They tried to provide him with ways out, but he resolutely refused to take them; on the contrary, he put himself into even deeper trouble with them—and with us.

If only he had backed down just a bit. It would have been much easier for his contemporaries and for us. But then of course, how can you back down when you are convinced that you can call God *Abba?* At times Jesus indicated that he would rather have liked the burden of his mission to pass from him; nonetheless he persisted. Great events were occurring, a sense of urgency was absolutely essential. He was conscious not merely of God's presence in loving intervention but he was conscious that God was present in *him.* It was not the urgency of threatened punishment; it was that of a splendid opportunity not to be missed. Why, oh why, did we not see how marvelous it was and how happy we would be if, like him, we dared to call the Father *Abba?* Even if we were prepared to accept the urgency of his message we seize upon passages in the New Testament which have some kind of an apocalyptic element in them to emphasize the urgency of escaping judgment instead of the urgency of accepting love. Jesus did not rule out judgment and punishment, nor did he deny apocalypse. (Much of the apocalypse in the New Testament apparently represents attempts by his followers to convey the eschatological, that is to say, the saving intervention, nature of Jesus' message.) But he was not primarily concerned with judgment or punishment and much less with the awful events of the Last Day. Indeed, he persistently refused to pay much attention to questions about when the End would come. He even made the scandalous statement that he did not know (a statement which scholars argue must be authentic because the New Testament writers would certainly not have permitted Jesus to utter something so scandalous unless he had beyond doubt said it). No, what Jesus was concerned with was the offer of love and the demand that we accept that offer.

But why can we not accept love? Perhaps because its demands never end. If this God of ours is so insanely generous, so passionately concerned with us, it is obvious that He never means to let us go. He will never leave us alone. We will never be able to do enough for Him. His affection for us will never stop. This Jesus whom He has sent is also a man who obviously makes immense demands. He constantly calls forth the very totality of our persons. And if we give ourselves over to these demands, what will we have left for ourselves? If we respond to a loving God and his challenging emissary, what will be left of us? They will consume us in their passion and their affection. They will never leave us alone, ever again. Isn't it enough that they created us, put us on this earth? Why can't they provide us with some sort of privacy, some opportunity to escape their insatiable demands for our affection? Why do they want us to be intimate with them? Why do they demand that we address them with the incredible term Abba? Wouldn't it be much better for all concerned if God and man were a little bit more formal, more restrained, more judicious, more stoical, or more platonic? If God were going to intervene in history, why didn't he choose the Greeks or Romans? They were rational people. But the Jews were crazy madmen, already engaged in a strange love affair with their rather odd God, Yahweh. They were perhaps the only race that could produce a bizarre notion of a God so intimately and familiarly available to all of us. As Hilaire Belloc put it, "How odd of God to choose the Jews."

Why was Jesus killed? In the final analysis, it was for the same reason that all great men are killed: they bother us. Jesus bothered us immensely. He bothered his contemporaries and he bothers us now. His contemporaries killed him, but he didn't even have the good taste to stay dead. He continues to bother us. We evade him, distort him, attempt to turn him into a preacher or a prophet, a political radical or a serene moralizer. But his authenticity and his integrity are too strong for our attempts to categorize him. He keeps breaking those bonds even as he broke out of the tomb. There he is again, still confronting us with the demand that we should believe in the kingdom of his Father; that we should address the Father, presumed head of the kingdom, with the same familiarity and affection, almost contempt, that he used.

Oh yes, indeed, it would be much better for all concerned if Jesus, the self-proclaimed Son of God, would go away. But he hasn't, and he won't, and he never will.

CHAPTER 6

JESUS THE MAN OF HOPE

The image of Jesus that many of us acquired in our early training frequently seems to reduce him to being a puppet. There was a scenario that the heavenly Father had designed. The role of Jesus had been written for him. He went onto the stage, played his part knowing exactly how it would all end, and departed to permit the rest of the drama to continue. In such a view of things there was little room in the life of Jesus for hope. He knew what was going to happen to him, he knew how the act would end, and how the drama would continue. Hope was no more pertinent an orientation for him than uncertainty of outcome would be for an actor in a play.

But such an image of Jesus has precious little to do with the reality of the New Testament. It is only by completely evading the evidence and distorting the language that we can conclude that Jesus was not hopeful.

But what is hope? It is the conviction, a modest conviction, that God is not mad—or, if one happens to be Christian, that God's insanity is benign. It is the belief, as Father Gregory Baum has expressed it, "that tomorrow will be different," or, as a young friend of mine has put it, "it is the assumption that the universe is out to do you good, and therefore it's all right to do good for yourself."

Ours is an age deeply concerned with hope. Because more than in any previous age we have a sense of history and of man's evolution, we are more concerned (pathologically so, perhaps) with the future than with the past. We are frequently aghast at the horrors and ugliness of the present in which man's capacity to do evil seems to have been multiplied one hundredfold by his new technological cleverness. Despite the ugliness of the present, we strive desperately to believe that the future will be better. The cult of science fiction among the young, the popularity of Father Teilhard among Catholics, the astrological conviction that the Age of Aquarius is dawning, Charles Reich's announcement of the advent of Consciousness III, the writings of the Marxist philosopher Bloch—all strive to obtain the conviction that despite all our trials and tribulations the human race is moving forward.

The trouble with many of these cosmic visions of hope is that there doesn't seem to be much room for the individual. The race will get better, the species will get better, the lot of the working class will improve, the third world will find abundance, America will eventually be green: these are exciting and challenging visions, particularly when one is young and expecting to see some of these visions come to fruition. But when one is older, he is not readily persuaded that these Splendid Days will dawn for him and that hope for the species which does not necessarily involve hope for himself seems rather empty and foul.

Jesus' message of hope is somewhat different in that it is much less future-oriented. The kingdom of God is yet to come in all its fullness. There will be an ultimate day of vindication. But the full message of Jesus is based on not so much the expectation of something that is yet to come as on the announcement and celebration of something already present.

As Christian Duquoc points out in a 1970 issue of *Concilium,* Jesus' hope will exist with the utter weakness of his personal situation. He refuses to display any sort of messianic strength. He does not work apocalyptic signs, he does not win great victories, he does not wield political power.

> The source of the revolution or the transformation of society would have been supernatural. It would not because of this ceased to be earthly. For the sign of his messianism would have been power, and to understand power does not demand a "conversion" of the heart. Jesus is dedicated to the very feeblest of means. To "convince" he has only his attitude and his word. This extreme weakness, this renouncement of all the apparatus of power even to allowing himself to be accused of imposture, are the sign of the greatest hope in God . . .[1]

Duquoc adds, "Jesus, Prophet and Revealer, assumes the risk of proclaiming the coming of the Kingdom in the feebleness of the Word. The risk was not imaginary: it was verified by his condemnation to death."[2]

Do not misunderstand this weakness of Jesus. This absolute and resolute refusal of his to yield to the messianic temptation is not naïve. He knows what is in man; he knows the scribes, the Pharisees, the Sadducees, the chief priests; he knows the fates of all the prophets; he knows what is going to happen to him.

> He pursues his path with no less audacity. Serene audacity, it is true. Patient audacity. He knows the stakes of his preaching. . . .

[1] Christian Duquoc, "The Hope of Jesus," *Concilium: Dimensions of Spirituality,* ed. by Christian Duquoc. New York: Herder and Herder, 1970, p. 26.
[2] *Ibid.,* p. 26.

> To found the Kingdom by power would have been to
> hide the face of God and to contradict the very meaning
> of Revelation. To found it in weakness and freedom was
> to take the risk of not seeing it come into being. Jesus
> enters actively into this risk. One person to sow and an-
> other to reap. God is faithful and it is in the "now" of
> this fidelity that the promised Kingdom is coming.[3]

One sees immediately the differences between this hope
and the hope we have discussed in previous paragraphs.
Jesus indeed believes that the universe is out to do us
good, but he feels no need to put constraints on the
Really Real—constraints that the exercise of power and the
working of signs would involve. He is so confident in
God that he can afford to be feeble and thereby give
the Really Real complete freedom to manifest his love for
us. Hope is based not on the evolution of the species or
on any action of man; neither is it to be found in some
strange mysticism inherent in the universe (either the Age
of Aquarius or Consciousness III). Hope and the dawning
age are the free and gratuitous loving intervention of the
Really Real. So powerful is this intervention that he who
manifests it can afford to appear weak and feeble. Jesus'
hope, as Duquoc tells us, is not based on blind optimism.
It is rooted in the experience of God present in him, loving
and transforming the world.

Jesus is therefore willing to wait. Instant victory is not
required. It is not necessary to force the hand of God or
to hasten the time of fulfillment of the kingdom. It is not
necessary to have a detailed timetable for the realization
of the kingdom. One does not have to supply answers to
questions of when and where and how. One does not expect to know exactly how the individual is to survive in
the kingdom that is simultaneously present and coming.

[3] *Ibid.,* p. 27.

It is sufficient merely to know that God loves. Man must have absolute trust in the power and goodness of this love. As Duquoc puts it:

> If Jesus' hope had been founded on an estimation of the evolution of societies, on an improvement in human relationships, it would only be optimism needing verification. It was never that and that is why he was able to risk everything so that eternal communion with God could be shared by men.[4]

Jesus was not a utopian or a dreamer. He did not deceive himself about the failure of his own preaching. He was angry at the stupidity of his audiences. He was pained by the pettiness of his disciples. Jesus was a deeply disappointed man, but none of his disappointment, none of his failure caused him to lose hope because, as Duquoc puts it, "the Kingdom is where there exists neither self-assessment nor demonstrations of power but communion with God."[5]

Note the great difference between Christian hope as manifested by Jesus and other forms of hope. The Marxist, for example, says that, even though the present state of society is unsatisfactory, the process is known by which society will evolve into a more perfect state, and his personal frustrations and disappointments will contribute to that evolutionary process. The apostle of Consciousness III declares that political action is not necessary, that all our discouragements need not be taken seriously because the messianic community—the youth culture—is already alive and ready to transform the world. In other words, one's hopes, disappointments, and discouragements are not seen

[4] *Ibid.*, p. 30.
[5] *Ibid.*, p. 30.

in these visions of hope as real. They are, rather, a part of the inevitable historical process tending toward victory.

But for Jesus and the Christian, defeats, failures, disappointments are very real indeed. One puts hope not in the collection of defeats culminating in victory but in the promise of the Father that victory is already present and will eventually manifest itself completely. Christian hope is frequently accused of promoting and fostering illusion, but the Christian is at least enough of a realist to recognize defeat and failure for what they are and not insist that they are part of some inevitable process toward victory. The Christian is also enough of a realist to be able to say that man left by himself has not been able to make the world a much better place. If love is to triumph eventually, some external force is going to have to intervene. Non-Christian hope still persistently believes, despite all evidence to the contrary, that we can do it alone.

Curiously enough, it is the Christian, precisely because he does not believe that a utopia will come by evolutionary process, who is more likely to sustain his commitment to the human condition. As Juan Alfaro says, "Man lives in so far as he has aspirations and plans, that is to say, in so far as he hopes."[6] But even if the non-Christian can deceive himself into believing that somehow the frustrations and uglinesses which he endures will contribute directly to some ultimate victory, he still must face the fact that he will not be around to enjoy the victory; for he must die. The awareness of death, that horrendous contradiction, demands consciousness of his own being. As Alfaro puts it:

In its very proximity to nothingness death is, thus, a frontier of the transcendent, a radical call to take the decision of hope. Being totally unable to render his existence

[6] Juan Alfaro, "Christian Hope and the Hopes of Mankind." *Concilium: Dimensions of Spirituality, op. cit.*, p. 59.

secure, man can only hope for the gift of a new existence. Death presents man with the option between an autonomous existence, limited to its possibilities in this world (a choice which is fundamental, whether it takes the form of heroic or fatalistic despair, of nausea at living, or an alienated existence ignoring death), and a brave open existence trusting in hope of a transcendent future. Death, then, is a frontier for man's freedom in the option it places before him between hoping and not hoping beyond the scope of this world. And because death is permanently present in human existence, the whole of life is a frontier of hope. In the response he makes to "transcendental hope" each individual interprets his own existence (every interpretation of one's own existence involves a choice) and decides its definitive meaning.[7]

In other words, when he is faced with the possibility of death, man has no choice but to face the fact that he is as weak and as feeble as Jesus was when he faced the envy of the Jewish leadership and the awesome power of Rome. Jesus refused to work signs and wonders; he refused to stop the sun or to call down the twelve legions of angels to protect him in his weak and feeble condition. We might very much like to do that when we are faced with death, but we are unable to do so. We are therefore forced to either give up hope or to accept the promise of a new existence as pure gift. The Christian by the very fact that he can transcend death with his expectation of such a pure gift is more likely to hope, more likely to have aspirations and plans, and more likely to be committed to life. Christian hope, Alfaro tells us, is an "exodus," that is, "a going out of oneself, renouncing any guarantee of salvation provided by human reckoning, in order to trust solely in the divine promise: a breaking of the moorings of all

[7] *Ibid.*, Alfaro, pp. 62–63.

assurance in oneself and in the world, and a tossing of the
anchor into the bottomless depths of the mystery of God
in Christ."[8] Yes, man hopes, and in the act of hoping he
experiences love by God. With that love he is possessed
by the certainty of the promise.

The Christian hope is not so much in an afterlife and
existence after existence; it is, rather, a hope in existence
itself: in the goodness and permanence of one's own being
rooted in God's promise. Even though Christians have frequently misunderstood this and acted as though they could
ignore their present existence in favor of some better existence to come, the fact is that Christian hope necessarily
commits the Christian to the fullness of his present in the
knowlege that God will transform it into a new existence.
In Alfaro's brilliant concluding paragraph, he says:

> Far from alienating man from his mission of transforming
> the world, Christian hope stimulates him to carry out his
> intramundane task and integrates his commitment to the
> world in his responsibility before God and before men, who
> are his brothers in the firstborn among men, Christ. The
> Christian lives according to the hope (founded in faith)
> that man's action in the world will neither end in failure
> nor lose itself in an endless search for a fulfilment which
> will never come; his hope in a definitive fulfilment sustains
> him in his worldly activity. Moreover, the grace of the
> Absolute Future does not remove but on the contrary rad-
> icalizes his responsibility as an actor with a part in history
> (just as the gift of justification does not suppress but is
> on the contrary fulfilled in the free response of faith); the
> salvation of man and of the world come about in the
> dialogue between the Absolute Freedom of God in his self-
> communication to man and man's responsible freedom before
> the call of the God-Love. Charity, the fullness of hope,
> demands from the Christian a radical involvement in the

[8] *Ibid.*, Alfaro, p. 67.

tasks of the world for the good of mankind. Precisely in the fulfilment of his responsibility to mankind, the world and history, Christian hope anticipates the coming of the Kingdom of God in Christ.[9]

The Christian, then, believes in failure just as Jesus believed in failure, but he knows that failure is not the end. He believes in fulfillment though he knows that he cannot achieve it himself. He knows that he is weak and will be defeated; but he knows that with God's help he can transcend that defeat to achieve victory. It is therefore impossible for him to quit; he cannot give up. When all around him have given up hope, the Christian, conscious of his feebleness and fragility, his weakness and his impotence, is still absolutely committed with the fullest confidence to the strength and love of God. When the charity of others runs out because of age, infirmity, discouragement or frustration, the Christian knows that this is not an option available to him. His hope demands that he continue working no matter how hopeless the situation.

There is a very fine line between the Christian's conviction that he must continue to work to humanize the world and the belief that his work will by itself accomplish that humanization. Hard work does not create the kingdom: it comes of itself through God's power in His own good time. Even the resurrection of Jesus could not cause the coming of the kingdom; it merely manifested it. We do not fully understand the complexity of things. We know that the kingdom is a gift, and we know that we must work toward it. We even understand that in some sense the kingdom is dependent upon our work and our response, though work and response will not cause it. So our effort matters. We commit ourselves to the works of justice and charity not just because we know that love will ultimately triumph be-

[9] *Ibid.*, Alfaro, p. 69.

cause of God's power but also because we understand that the triumph of love works somehow or other through us even though we are not its principal cause. The Christian cannot afford the luxury of relaxing and waiting for God to do everything. Jesus *cared*. He cared deeply and profoundly despite the fact that he knew the kingdom was to come inevitably. In the final analysis, to reconcile our care and commitment, on the one hand, with the inevitability of the coming of the kingdom, on the other, is beyond our human powers of comprehension. We do at least understand this, it is practically impossible to sustain care and commitment in the face of discouragement and the prospect of death unless one is able to believe in the coming of something which transcends us and our efforts.

The tension between the free coming of the kingdom and our own effort is a hard one to balance. I remember giving a lecture at a meeting of college chaplains in which I suggested that the campus ministry could expect to have little direct impact on the life of the university and that therefore what the campus clergy and their flocks should strive to do is to create a model of human relationships of love and trust which would be a light on the mountain to which the rest of the campus could look if they wished. One of the Protestant clergymen present was highly irate. I was preaching a form of Pietism, I was arguing for irrelevance and justifying a cop-out from the demands for involvement. He was astonished that a social scientist could possibly think that faith and love were enough to change American higher education.

I responded that, as a sociologist, I was astonished that he thought anything else would change American education. Furthermore, my social scientific analysis of the role of the church on campus led me to believe that in terms of any direct action toward reform the campus chaplain and his flock could count on nothing more than marginal effectiveness.

His reply was that at least at his university this was not true. He had attended faculty meetings and marched on picket lines; he served on committees promoting educational reform. He was making the Christian voice heard in these situations. Alas, anyone who knows higher education knows that nothing ever happens in committees or at faculty meetings, and that picket lines generally affect only symptoms and not causes. My Protestant minister friend was totally irrelevant to the life of the campus. His frantic efforts to attain relevance by compulsive activity were bound to end in frustration and defeat.

We must, of course, work for higher educational reform. We must, I suppose, go to meetings and even occasionally march on picket lines. But we deceive ourselves if we think these activities are nearly as effective as the witness of a life of commitment, confidence, trust, and love. I hope higher education can be reformed eventually. (Although I really don't see how. I think it may take some special interventions from the heavenly Father to really stir this most recalcitrant of institutions.) I know that if it is ever to be reformed by men, they must be men whose confidence and hope are rooted in something much deeper than attending faculty meetings, marching in picket lines, or participating in the latest campus crisis. Nothing is more hilarious six months after the Kent State-Cambodia demonstrations than to read the apocalyptic articles in the divinity school journals. Such great hope was placed in the fervor of the May moment, and but a half year later, that ferment has been poured down the sink like stale beer. The good divines on these faculties would have been better advised to root their hope in something more permanent, to work with the serence confidence of men who need not see results to have their hope confirmed, who need not exercise power to be confident of the coming and presence of the kingdom, who need not feel strength to know that they labor not in vain, who can experience frustration and discouragements as painful but not ultimate conditions.

On another occasion I was asked to give a speech about the future of religion in the contemporary world. I suggested that its future was probably as secure as its past, because men were not likely to stop asking those questions about meaning they had asked since thought began. Indeed, it seemed to me that the crises of the present days were, if anything, driving men to ask more explicitly and more vigorously the questions of meaning which are at the core of any human value system. After my talk the Methodist cleric who had convened the conference (to force the churches to "take a stand on social issues," as it turned out) announced that we heard too much about faith and not enough about action, and that it was time for the churches to go on record as favoring action.

I certainly would not want to oppose the churches' going on record in favor of action, but what happens after they are on the record and the pace of social change does not accelerate? I wonder if my Methodist friend would then begin to consider the possibility that resolutions at the end of meetings are relatively meaningless, and that social action commitments without a profound transformation of one's world view are likely to turn sour. That social change in the long run is likely to be accomplished not so much by men who insist on immediate action but by men who are deeply committed to faith and see the pertinence of that faith to the agonies of the human condition. To repeat a theme I mentioned in the previous chapter, the commitment of the Christian is such that he realizes that discouragement is simply a luxury he cannot afford, at least not for very long. Quitting is a self-indulgence that he cannot permit himself. Even if he knows he is going to lose now, he knows that in the long run he will win. Jesus knew he would lose; he did not stop trying or caring. He was able to sustain his effort only because he also knew that through the power of his heavenly Father he would eventually win.

The commitment to the notion that the world is out to do us good and in the long run we will win is also absolutely essential if one is not to turn away in terror from the paralyzing fear of giving oneself to others. Josef Goldbrunner says:

> To surrender myself, to put myself defenseless into someone else's hands in total trust, to do this at the risk of being exploited and misused, all this grows into a true experience of dying as we grow older. The sudden changeover to a life with a new quality, the personal quality, is only possible by dying to the protective armour-plated world we have built around ourselves. A person who does not give his self away cannot break through his isolation, nor escape from the prison of meaninglessness, cannot open up, trust, ask, forgive, love.
>
> Change, metamorphosis, renewal, resurrection—all these words picture what happens when an event bursts upon us and calls us forth, and the answer is not given by reason or some emotion, but by the personal self. This centre of my self is called upon, and then actuated and shaped by the response to this call. "Above" and "below" find themselves united again in me in a new way.[10]

In despair, one faces the certainty of failure in one's efforts to change the world and the experience of terror at being cut off from others. To maintain commitment in the face of frustration, to take risks in the face of terror, requires a profound conviction that the world is indeed out to do you good. Personal existence, whether manifested in personal responsibility for the world or in discovering the lost dimension of ourselves and radiating it to others, re-

[10] Josef Goldbrunner, "What is Despair?" *Concilium, op. cit.,* pp. 74-75.

quires the absolute confidence that defeat or rejection is
not ultimate and that though our plans fail and our
friends spurn and reject us, tomorrow we will be different.
I am not suggesting that Christians have a monopoly on
this conviction. Men sustain effort and faith in the face of
discouragement and continue to break through the armor
plate of their defensiveness without the benefit of the full
and explicit Christian message. I am asserting that he who
does possess that message is better equipped to sustain
hope because he has complete confidence in final victory
and final resurrection. But one must say more than that. It
is not merely that hope ought to be more possible for a
Christian; it is also more necessary for him. The existential
commitment that he makes demands that he be hopeful. In
Alfaro's epigram " 'Justification by faith' means 'salvation in
hope'."[11] The Christian who is not a man of hope stands
revealed as not being a man of faith. Hope is a necessary
though always difficult and painful consequence of the
commitment of faith. Hope is not only a possibility for us;
it is in the final analysis an obligation.

One of my agnostic colleagues summarized his theology
this way: "God created man and grew very dissatisfied with
man's evil. Therefore, He condemned man to hell, which is
the situation in which we presently live. Then God took
pity upon us and permitted us to escape this hell—by
death."

I am not sure that my friend fully believes this theology.
He does not, it seems to me, live by it, but, in any event,
a man who truly accepts that view of the universe is surely
not hypocritical when he gives up his efforts to reform the
world or when he quits trying to break through the barriers
of fear and suspicion that separate him from other human
beings. Indeed, quitting, giving up, waiting for the liberation of death, is perfectly consistent with his position. But
the opposite position, which I take to be that of the Chris-

11 Alfaro, op. cit., p. 67.

tian, is the one manifested by Jesus of Nazareth. Because
we believe in the presence of the kingdom, because we
believe that we do have the privilege and the obligation to
call God Abba, because we are fully conscious of our own
weakness we continue to plug away. Indeed, one might
even say, plug *merrily* away, because we know the future
to be ours.

It has often seemed to me that if the Really Real did
want to communicate with us, He selected in the symbol
of Jesus an extraordinarily effective means. Sometimes we
would think that the Real would have been better advised
to produce active signs and wonders, but, as Father Duquoc
mentioned in his aforementioned article, that would have
been to compromise the fundamental nature of the message
that he apparently wished to communicate to us.

Given the constraints under which, for reasons of His
own, the Real chose to operate, He did come up with a
marvelously effective symbol. But the symbol hasn't worked
for most of us, or at least it has worked poorly. In some
sense the Real must be criticized for this—not so much for
putting together a bad symbol but for choosing to create
and to bother with such a stubborn and thickheaded crea-
ture which has developed such incredible skill at ignoring,
evading, misunderstanding, and misinterpreting perfectly
good religious symbols.

The Bethlehem symbol, to which we turn each year at
Christmas, is one whose persistence and power man could
never have expected. Granted, of course, that the Bethlehem
scene cannot be reduced to scientific history like some of
the other sections of the gospel. Nonetheless, according to
the most recent scholars, it is part of a very ancient tradition which goes back to Palestine in the decade immediately after the death and resurrection of Jesus. The secret
of the power of the Bethlehem symbol is the extraordinarily
ingenious combination of power and weakness, or, to use
Cardinal Newman's words, "omnipotence in bonds." And

yet, on a priori grounds, who would have thought that the image of a man, a woman, and a child in a cave with animals and shepherds hovering in the background could possibly have any religious significance? Many hundreds of thousands of times the scene must have been re-enacted in the course of human history. People could pass by and not even notice save for a brief moment of compassion for a mother and child in such uncomfortable circumstances. Yet the scene has exercised a magnetic attraction for almost two millennia, and it has survived all the vulgar commercialism of our own time as well as the phony joy of so many Christmas celebrations. It has survived precisely because its very commonness, its very ordinariness, its very universality make it such a powerful and appealing message of hope. The Bethlehem scene is nothing more than that fundamental message of Jesus reduced to a setting we can all understand and with which we can all identify. Bethlehem stands for hope because it conveys the message that God loves us so much that we can find Him manifested in the mystery of human life in the most ordinary and commonplace circumstances. Jesus was a man of hope because he was completely committed to the message he preached —a message symbolized for us by the Bethlehem scene. Those of us who claim to be followers of Jesus have no choice but to live in the same hope. And for us, alas, the Christmas symbol is more than just a charming sign of God's love, more than just evidence of the power of the Real to inspire us to heights of poetic imagery. It is a demand that if we take the symbol seriously we can never permit ourselves the delightful melancholy cynicism of despair.

CHAPTER 7

THAT HIS WILL MIGHT BE DONE

In the Lord's Prayer, the kingdom of the Father and His will are different aspects of the same reality. The kingdom is God's loving intervention in human history. His will is that man responds to that invitation. He must respond first by accepting the gift and then by giving a life which will manifest the kingdom of God with a light shining on the mountaintop.

We noted previously that Jesus did not come specifically to preach a new ethic; he came to proclaim a kingdom. He also made it clear that we would know the members of the kingdom by the way they lived. Jesus' attitude toward ethics and morality is nicely illustrated by his reaction to the Jewish law. His condemnation is not so much the essence of the law itself, particularly as it is manifested in the Decalogue, but rather the juridic, legalistic interpretations which had been fastened on it like a straitjacket.

Those who have made the existential leap of commitment in accepting the kingdom of the Father are not held to the narrow legalistic interpretation of the law; they are held to something far more difficult: the spirit of the law. They cannot manifest the kingdom by simply asserting that they have fulfilled a certain number of highly specific, neatly codified, and exhaustively listed regulations. It is not enough that they avoid murder, which is relatively easy;

they must respect one another, which is very difficult. It is not enough to avoid adultery, which is moderately difficult; they must preserve in marriage a reverence and respect for one's spouse, which is extremely difficult. It is not enough to guarantee one's truthfulness by swearing an oath; one must also guarantee it by being so transparent that an oath becomes unnecessary. It is not only enough to love one's friends, one must also love one's enemies.

But it is also not enough to reduce chastity and charity and honesty and patience and respect to juridic categories —as we Christians have all too frequently done. Gunther Bornkamm points out that obedience to the law as Jesus enunciated it is not something measurable, something that can be demonstrated, something that can be subject to reckoning, and counter-reckoning, to merit and debt, to the economics of double-entry bookkeeping.[1] The will of God is not that we pile up merit for ourselves or that we honor specific, neatly delineated rules which apply to all circumstances. What is necessary, rather, is that we live the kinds of lives of openness and love which will demonstrate that we have indeed responded positively to the challenge of the kingdom which Jesus proclaimed.

Jesus wants no part of legalism. He rejected the legalism of the Pharisees, and there is no reason to think that he expected his followers to engage in newer and higher levels of Pharisaism. Bornkamm notes:

> . . . the words of Jesus in their concreteness have nothing to do with the casuistry of Jewish legalism. Characteristic of this legalism is its endeavour to enmesh man's whole life ever more tightly. With each new mesh, however, it forms a new hole, and in its zeal to become really specific it in reality fails to capture the human heart. This "heart-

[1] Gunther Bornkamm, *Jesus of Nazareth*. Translated by Irene and Fraser McLuskey with James M. Robinson. New York: Harper & Row, 1960.

lessness" is characteristic for all casuistry. The concrete
directions of Jesus, however, reach through the gaps and
holes for the heart of man and hit their mark where his
existence in relation to his neighbour and to his God is
really at issue.[2]

Yet, Christianity has not been free, to put the matter mildly,
of those who have instituted a "higher grade of Pharisaism,
more rigorous and more painstaking even than that of
Jesus' adversaries."[3]

In *The Sermon on the Mount*, Joachim Jeremias notes
that there have been two misunderstandings of the "ethics"
enunciated in the Sermon.[4] I will call one misunderstanding
"Catholic" and the other "Protestant." The Catholic misunderstanding is to see the ethical ideal laid down by the
Sermon as a counsel of moral perfection rather than a strict
moral imperative. Those who wish to or are able to are
strongly encouraged to live by the Sermon on the Mount,
but it is not expected of all men.

According to the "Protestant" aberration, the Sermon is
indeed a description of a strict moral imperative, but one
which man cannot possibly respond to. Therefore, when
faced with both the imperative and his own weakness, man
has no choice but to throw himself to the mercy of God and
plead for forgiveness for his inadequacy.

Both interpretations assume that Jesus is in fact laying
down an ethical code, more noble indeed than that of the
Pharisees, but fundamentally a code demanding maximum
effort to see that each of its regulations is honored. But, as
Jeremias observes, if we look at the life described in the
Sermon on the Mount in its proper context, it does not
represent an ethical code at all. It is a description of an

[2] *Ibid.*, pp. 105–6.
[3] *Ibid.*, p. 107.
[4] Joachim Jeremias, *The Sermon on the Mount*. Translated by Norman
Perrin. Facet Books, Biblical Series—2. Philadelphia: Fortress Press, 1963.

eschatological reality.[5] The "hunger" and "thirst" are not physical; they are a yearning for God's kingdom. The "mourning" is not for earthly suffering but for the fact that the kingdom has not yet been fulfilled completely. So the Sermon on the Mount is a description of how those who respond positively to the invitation of the kingdom will be able to live. They will be the "light of the world" and "the salt of the earth" precisely because their happiness, their love, their freedom, and their joy will make them new kinds of men—men of truthfulness, generosity, patience, chastity, and goodness.

The Sermon on the Mount does not present a moral or ethical code that must be adopted to earn entrance into the kingdom. It is rather the way those who have decisively chosen for the kingdom will in fact behave—not always, of course, and not perfectly, surely, but at least consistently enough so that the whole quality and tenor of their lives will be demonstrably different from that of those who have not yet committed themselves to the kingdom. Bornkamm describes this "new righteousness" as a qualitatively new and different attitude.

> The truth is that the new righteousness is qualitatively a new and different attitude. In accordance with the biblical idiom elsewhere, neither the concept "righteousness" nor that of "perfection" could be exceeded. "You, therefore, must be perfect, as your heavenly Father is perfect" (Mr. v.48). This is not an ideal which may be achieved step by step, but means "wholeness" in comparison with all dividedness and brokenness; a state of being, a stance whose reality is in God. In the demand which he makes upon them, Jesus points the disciples, with the greatest emphasis, to God—the God who will come and is already

[5] Indeed, Luke's version of the Beatitudes with which the Sermon begins is clearly an eschatological variant of St. Matthew's more catechetical version. Most authors think Luke's Sermon on the Plain is an earlier form of the Sermon on the Mount.

present and active. To live on the basis of God's presence
and in expectation of his future, this is what Jesus aims
at in his commandment: "That you may be the children
of your Father who is in Heaven!"[6]

In a strange paradox, those who have committed themselves to doing God's will are both liberated from the world,
since they no longer feel tied to onerous and legalistic regulations, and at the same time put back into the world in the
sense that their lives now make them "a light on the mountaintop" and the "salt of the earth." The Sermon on the
Mount is not a program for legislative and social reform.
It is a description of a life style by which we will know
those who have accepted God's kingdom; a life style which
flows, albeit not easily, from the joy and happiness and love
which one experiences when one has decisively responded
to the invitation to the wedding feast. The Sermon on the
Mount, then, describes a mode of conduct for the eschatological banquet. It portrays the way guests will act at the
splendid party to which God has invited them. Why must
one love other men, even those who are enemies, even
those who are Samaritans? The reason is quite simple. As
Bornkamm notes: "The ground of his command of love is
simply because it is what God wills and what God does."[7]
The fact that love has no limits does not mean that all the
boundaries among men are eliminated. The frontiers between friend and foe, Jew and Samaritan, neighbor and
stranger, Pharisee and tax collector still exist, but God's
love is not limited by those boundaries, and neither must
ours. God is so insanely generous as to permit His rain to
fall gently on the crops of both the good and the wicked.
He refuses to distinguish between His friends and enemies;
and we have no right to make such distinctions in our love
either.

[6] Bornkamm, *op. cit.*, p. 108.
[7] *Ibid.*, p. 114.

The Sermon on the Mount, as we have said before, does not provide a blueprint for remaking the world. It does describe a life style, a mode of relating to our fellow men without which the world will never be remade. The world has not yet been remade, not because the Sermon on the Mount is inadequate or too lofty as an ideal but because the commitment to faith which it presupposes has not been made completely and totally enough by very many people. As G. K. Chesterton put it, "it is not that it has been tried and found wanting, it has been found hard and not tried."

And if we do not see many Christians whose relationships with their fellows do act like the "light on the mountaintop" described in the Sermon, if there are not many Christians whose behavior is like that of the good Samaritan, then the reason is not that Christianity has failed or that the ethical ideal of love laid down in the Sermon on the Mount and the parable of the Good Samaritan is inadequate. The reason is simply that there haven't been very many Christians.

Juridicism, whether it be of the "Catholic" or "Protestant" variety, is a manifestation of the same pervasive human temptation to which the Pharisees succumbed: the temptation to insist on the letter as a substitute for the spirit, to feel that morality can be reduced to doing certain things instead of a way to do all things. We have vigorously and more or less successfully ignored Jesus' teaching in this respect, and in many cases succeeded in out-Phariseeing the Pharisees in evolving a vast complex of moral obligation, some binding under "mortal sin," some under "venial sin," and some simply binding under the pain of being guilty of "imperfection." This approach to morality is perhaps being left behind; yet one wonders how in view of the Sermon on the Mount it could ever have been taken seriously. I am not at all persuaded that a new "liberal" or "existential" or "psychological" juridicism will not replace the old moral theology juridicism. There are certain kinds of behavior, for example, which are as rigidly prescribed by sensitivity and encounter groups as were other norms of behavior prescribed in days gone past by novice masters and mistresses. The Pharisees we always have with us, even if now some of them appear in the guise of T-group leaders.

I am not arguing for the abolition of moral systems. Jesus didn't argue that either. As he pointed out, he came not to abolish the law but to fulfill it. Man cannot do without moral systems, without ethical codes, for *ethos*, as Clifford Geertz tells us, is but the other side of the coin of *mythos*. Man's conception of how the good man behaves is but a reflection of his concept of what Reality really is. Even the "situationists" or the "contextualists" end up almost necessarily with some new form of systematic morality, though usually one which takes a more benign view of sexual aberrations than the older systems—a view which is in its turn often rooted in a simpleminded misunderstanding of psychoanalysis.

For some strange, perverse reason there has always been a tendency to believe that liberation from moral juridicism means that man has greater freedom to engage in illicit behavior; that he is no longer constrained to be good. But Jesus insisted on liberating his followers from the legalism of the Torah not so that they were now free of sin but so they were free to be good. Moral systems are not thereby abolished. They are seen as being quite incapable of providing "righteousness." They may be necessary, useful, helpful guides, but by themselves they do not provide the good life, and honoring them to the letter is not a sign that one has acted decisively in favor of the kingdom. The liberation implicit in the Sermon on the Mount is less a liberation from an obligation to honor minutiae as it is a liberation for practicing love even in situations where a moral code provides no strict and explicit regulations. To do God's will means to love our neighbor in the concrete circumstances in which we find him. A moral system can be an extremely helpful guideline as to what we ought to do in those concrete circumstances, but those who are part of the kingdom will not point with pride to their implementation of the strict literal norms of the moral system as evidence that they are indeed acting like "lights on the mountaintop."

From one point of view we can say that Jesus' whole ministry was an effort to persuade men that they could find security nowhere else save in God. The difficulty with the rich young man was not so much that his riches were evil, but that he sought his own personal security from them. But if there are dangers from riches, there is certainly no automatic justification from poverty. The poor man was more likely to hunger and thirst after God's kingdom because he was not able to afford the luxury of the rich man's thinking he could find security in his wealth. But neither can security be found in poverty, which no more justifies a man than riches consoles him. We can only find salvation by accepting God's love and responding to it. Honoring the explicit, specific regulations of a moral law does not justify us; poverty does not justify us; giving alms to the poor does not justify us; striving to become virtuous by our own unaided efforts does not justify us: only by God's love are we justified. Only when we decisively accept that love and respond to it with the same almost mad generosity that characterizes His love for us can we feel secure. Indeed, the love of God and love of neighbor cannot be separated. As Jesus insists in the twenty-fifth chapter of St. Matthew, "What we do to others, we do to God." We cannot respond positively to God's love for us unless we manifest that love to the least of our brothers. It is not an indirect love achieved by a detour through our love of God; it is, quite the contrary, an overflowing of God's love accepted by us and radiating out from us to all with whom we come into contact. Once we permit God's love to operate in us, our own love floods out and engulfs others.

There is something of a mutual causality at work here.

We cannot love others, at least not in the way described by Jesus as the will of his heavenly Father, unless we first accept God's love for us; and in the very act of loving others we experience that love yet more deeply. The very difficulty we experience in loving the very least of our brothers forces us back upon the love of God. And in that deepening understanding of His love, we turn with love toward our brothers once again.

All of this has precious little to do with the juridicism of the Pharisees and the novice masters, of moral theology books, and of catechisms. But neither has it much to do with the sloppy sentimentality of those contextualists who are bent on justifying premarital sex at any cost. The will of the heavenly Father as described in the Sermon on the Mount, the parable of the Good Samaritan, and in Matthew 25 is not terribly concerned with what we can't do or what we can do. Virtue is not achieved in that fashion. The will of the heavenly Father is rather that we love even as we are loved; that we be as generous to others as God is to us. Such a position is neither juridic nor sentimental; it demands the courage, persistence, tenacity, and generosity that can only be sustained by a man filled with hope and quite conscious of being passionately loved.

Another of Jesus' sayings, that about paying tribute to Caesar, bears directly on this point. Jesus was asked a political question; he gave an eschatological answer. The point was not (at least not principally) that it was moral to pay taxes to political authority. The emphasis is not on rendering to Caesar those things that are Caesar's but rather on rendering to God those things that are God's. Once again, Jesus refused to be trapped by the perspectives of his questioners. It was not so much that the political issue was unimportant as it was that it was rather less important than the message he had come to preach. If men paid taxes to political regimes, however grudgingly, how much more they were held to the requirements of God. Caesar wanted taxes, so give him taxes. God wants love, your love; therefore, render to him that love he has the right to require. Caesar is satisfied with the payment of coin. It is not that simple with God. He does not want specific actions from you. He wants *you*.

There have been a few people in the course of history who have ridiculed the Sermon on the Mount, seeing in it a surrender of the dignity and integrity of the individual, the destruction of man's will to live by a God who wishes to reduce man to a state of total dependency. Such a view may have given nineteenth-century German philosophers a chance to work out some of their personality problems, but it is obvious, I trust, that it is based on a fundamental misunderstanding of the will of God as described in the New Testament. We are not called to surrender our vigor or our strength. We are urged, rather, to exercise them in making a decisive commitment and then in living the life that commitment makes possible for us. Almost two millennia of sermons may have made the vision of the Sermon on the Mount seem weak and effeminate. Being a "light on the mountaintop" is no great challenge to us when it seems vague, shallow, "pious," and unhuman. Just as we convert Jesus into a nice, simple, moral teacher to avoid having to face what he really was, so we turn his moral code either into an impossible ideal or a manifestation of a passive, dependent personality. Then we can easily dismiss it; we will not have to face Jesus' insistent demand that we love even as we are loved.

I trust that the reader will excuse me for quoting one more question after a lecture. (Lecture questions seem to embody in the purest form possible the evasions we have developed for ourselves.) Speaking to a group of educators, I once noted that it seemed to me that the educational experience was most effective when the process was marked by love between teacher and student and among students. After the talk, one black educator rose demanding to know whether I was saying that black students should love white teachers and white administrators after the centuries of tyranny, oppression, and suffering they had endured from the white man. I could have said that black students today have not endured centuries of suffering and oppression since they haven't lived that long, or I could have asked whether he thought those of Irish background should hate professors of English background, especially since the Irish died during the potato famine in far greater numbers than the blacks did at any time of their white domination. But these would have been *ad hominem* arguments which only indicate the foolishness of hatred.

I replied by saying that the only answer I knew was that of a Christian. If hatred could be justified, a convincing case could be made for blacks hating their white oppressors. But, as a Christian, I did not believe that hate could ever be justified. Many of the blacks in the audience and some of the liberals violently disagreed. Only by hating, they argued, could the black man be free. Only, in other words, by reacting to white men as white men had reacted to them could the black man escape the results of the white man's hatred. Those senseless and foolish humanists! Hatred merely breeds further hatred, and no one in human history has ever become free by hating. Does it impose a heavy burden on black men to ask that they love white men? Of course it does. But the demand to love is a great imposition on anyone. And Jesus leaves no doubt that responding to the love of his heavenly Father necessarily impels us to love others. The Samaritan should have hated the Jew, but that wouldn't have made him any more free of the Jew, it wouldn't have made him any more proud to be a Samaritan. He would not have been able to go back to Samaria proclaiming that "Samaritan is beautiful." His hatred would have made him no better a human being than he was before encountering the Jew and no better than the Jew who hated him. The Christian may well be able to understand why men hate, but, given his commitment, it is something he cannot accept for himself or approve as a political or social strategy.

In the dark, passionate, romantic period in which we presently find ourselves, hatred is fashionable again. Anti-Semitism has reared its ugly head under the guise of anti-Zionism. The counterculture urges the young to hate the old and their Establishment. Black extremists urge their compatriots to hate whity, and white militants pursue their own policies of vengeful hatred. Young radicals are urged to hate and, if necessary, to destroy their enemy. International congresses of Catholic theologians adopt resolutions endorsing the actions of revolutionaries who want to deprive other men of their freedom and their lives. Women's liberation in some of its forms actively urges women to hate men, and the white liberals encourage, and even on occasion demand, that young blacks manifest hatred for whites.

All of this hatred is justified in terms of being necessary that men might be free. It seems incredible that after all the years of bitter experience the race has not yet learned that hatred never frees anyone. Presumably, our present romantic era will end, and we will recognize once again that hatred is no solution. So it will be put aside or repressed into our unconscious, and we will pretend again to love. But it will be a careful, antiseptic love, even among most of us Christians. We are, of course, prepared to love our fellows, but to love with the same generosity that God gave to us through Jesus is simply not possible.

That is correct. It is not possible—not unless we have already made the decisive commitment to accept with joy and celebration God's love for us.

CHAPTER 8

THE DISCIPLES

Jesus came to invite all men to the wedding feast. The Good News was for everyone. Those who accepted his invitation would live lives of love which would make them the salt of the earth and the light of the world. All those who responded to his invitation would be his followers.

But also within the band of followers there was a special group: his immediate followers, his disciples. It is clear from the New Testament that Jesus did have such a select group of intimate followers; but it is difficult for us to sort out which of his instructions were specifically for them and which were aimed at all his followers. There are two reasons for this difficulty. The first is that Jesus himself apparently drew no firm line of distinction between the two groups. Furthermore, the early Church, in recounting Jesus' words and deeds, frequently made use of the stories to reinforce and emphasize certain points of Christian beliefs that were pertinent to the situation for which the writers of the New Testament were directing their books. Jesus' chiding the disciples for their lack of faith, for example, must be understood as a story told not so much to recount Jesus' actual words to his disciples but to use Jesus' words to chide some segments of the early Christian community for their lack of faith.

Nevertheless, it is clear that there were some men who

were assigned special roles. They did not choose their roles, they were chosen by Jesus. They were called to come after him with a special call not received by others. They had to be prepared to leave behind their ordinary lives. They were expected to be as mobile as Jesus without necessarily finding a place on which to lay their heads. They had no reason to think that their faith would be any different from the faith of Jesus or that they would receive any more acceptance than he did. They were advised to reckon costs carefully in responding to the special invitation. It was not wise for them to be rash. If they were to build towers, they should have enough money to finish them lest they be mocked by their friends. If they were going to war, they would be sure to have an army strong enough to win; therefore, if they were going to follow Jesus, they must be sure that they knew what they were getting into and that they were willing to pay the price.

But the demands being made on the special disciples was not a new moral code designed for a hand-picked elite. It was not an ascetic ideal which Jesus demanded from a precious few. They were called not to be ascetics, not simply to be holy men; they were called upon to help Jesus to proclaim the kingdom of God. And it is the kingdom, this eschaton, this special intervention of God in history, that is the only foundation of the call. In Bornkamm's words:

> The special demand made upon the disciples must, therefore, not be understood at all as a moral code for an elite, as a proclamation of an ascetic ideal which Jesus exacts only from the few, little as he elsewhere rejects earthly things as such: vocation and property, sex, marriage, and family. The kingdom of God is the sole foundation of Jesus' call to follow him. It imposes upon the disciples a special task, a special destiny, but also grants them a special promise.[1]

[1] Bornkamm, *op. cit.*, p. 148.

The task of the apostles' was to to be fishers of men. But they are fishers not by trapping or cajoling, much less by tyrannizing them. Rather, they proclaim the victory of the kingdom; they are called to share the healing power, the authority, and the triumph of Jesus, but they must be prepared to share his suffering and his death.

As Father Raymond Brown points out in his splendid little book on the priesthood, *Priest and Bishop,* we cannot make an automatic transition from the apostles and the Old Testament to the bishops and priests of today. The evolution of the Christian ministry to its present form was more complicated even in the first century. Nevertheless, the priest today in the present state of the Church is expected to play a role roughly equivalent to that of the disciple as described in the New Testament. (Though the priest may not be the only one called upon to play such a role.)

A Catholic theologian writing in the magazine *Commonweal* suggested that, since the sacred was no longer a useful category in the human experience, there was obviously no meaningful distinction between priests and lay persons in the Church and that therefore the title "priest" ought to be abolished. The death of the sacred, it turns out, was premature, as *Commonweal* itself announced about a year after. But the title "priest" is not at all indispensable. Father Brown suggests that in New Testament days the one who presided over the Eucharist was not necessarily the one who was the *presbyter-episcopos.* Neither of these two roles was the same as the role of the apostles. One could, perhaps, separate the roles again. But the important point is not what we call him or what his task is. The point is that one can scarcely think of a community of Jesus' followers without thinking of some people exercising the role of disciple, that is to say, of the immediate follower who has a special challenge and commission to proclaim the kingdom—a challenge and commission which he has not chosen, but for which he has been chosen.

As we will note in a later chapter, Jesus did not devote himself to the founding of the Church in the sense that he laid out a neat organizational plan or, much less, that he had tucked away in the back of his head the schema of the code of canon law. Jesus came to proclaim the kingdom and to summon men to follow after him in that kingdom. He was well aware that those who believed his message would form a community. He did found a church in the sense that his message and his instructions provided a mandate for that community.

Jesus would certainly not have approved of hard and fast caste distinctions between those who would play the role roughly equivalent to the fishers of men and others in the community, for all were to be lights on the mountaintop and salt of the earth. But it is hard to read the New Testament and escape the conclusion that there were some men in his community who would be chosen by him for a special mission. The significant thing about the disciple was not his special position and surely not his assumption of moral excellence. The important thing was the proclamation of the kingdom: to proclaim the insane generosity of God and the fabulous marriage feast to which all had been invited. The disciples were marked as men not merely by the quality of their lives but also by active and presumably full-time preaching of the Good News.

That priests—of whom it can be said they are officially commissioned to the role of discipleship—and laity might be restless and dissatisfied with the way this special mandate had been institutionalized in the pre-Vatican Church is surely understandable. In the layman's point of view, priests were a separate caste having all the power and the privilege in the Church. From the priest's point of view, he was cut off not only from his people but also from the human condition. But railing against transitory institutional structures ought not to lead us to overlook the fact that the notion of a special call to some men to devote their lives to the proclamation of the kingdom is unquestionably rooted in the New Testament. As Father Brown vigorously notes, "Can we overlook the fact that the New Testament leaves no doubt at all that these special followers of Jesus are called to a life of extreme dedication and sacrifice?" The dedication is of course not tied to any specific norms. As we know by now, Jesus wanted no part of juridic categories. It is not legitimate, for example, to say that one man is a good disciple because he owns a Volkswagen and another man a bad disciple because he owns a Pontiac, and yet another man is the best of the lot because he only owns a Schwinn bicycle. Such moralistic categorizing, so immensely popular for two millennia of Christian history, is completely foreign to the message of Jesus. Forms of dedication to the proclamation of the kingdom, to the heralding of the wedding feast, will change in time and place. Celibacy, for example, may be an extremely helpful asset to the disciple. Father Brown goes so far as to suggest that one could make a strong case from the New Testament that the Church has the right to require this of those who play the disciple role. But while the Church may decide to require it at certain times and certain places, and may even legitimately do so, it does not follow that Jesus has specified it as essential for his closest followers. They must simply be ready to follow him wherever he calls, indeed, follow him enthusiastically. What this means concretely in given situations is something that Jesus leaves to those who came after him; he refuses to legislate himself.

A lay reader of this chapter might well wonder why there is such confusion and uncertainty in the clergy about the role of the priest. The New Testament makes it clear that the disciple is one who is to dedicate his life to the explicit proclamation of the kingdom. Why isn't it clear to many troubled clergymen that that indeed is their role, even if they have other roles in addition, such as administering the Church's communal affairs and presiding over

the Eucharist? (One can view the presidency of the
Eucharist, of course, as at the very core of the proclamation mission.) If the disciple is really to do the same thing
Jesus did, then why doesn't the priest understand that his
task is to announce to all that there is a wedding feast
being convened, a banquet being assembled, a splendid
party just getting under way, and that everyone should
come to the party before it is too late?

St. John's narrative of the life of Jesus begins, we are
told, with an account of the marriage feast at Cana because
John wants to emphasize the festive nature of the proclamation of Jesus. Why don't priests understand, then? They
are indeed celebrants, men whose role it is to announce
and preside over a festive celebration.

One of the reasons, I suspect, is that the role model of
the priesthood that was provided for us in our training
said very little about festivity and celebration and practically nothing about zeal for proclaiming the kingdom. In
all my years at the seminary I heard countless talks on
the necessity for obedience to the will of God (always
interpreted for us by the pastor). I cannot recall a single
talk about zeal. I was warned repeatedly about the loneliness
and difficulty of the priestly life (though I don't know that
I have ever felt particularly lonely, save for a couple of
days when I found myself marooned in Istanbul), but no
one ever suggested to me that I was supposed to announce
and preside over a splendid celebration.

What happened, of course, was that because the Church
could not really be sure of the internal convictions of its
clergy, it decided to settle for external conformity. If we
were not really to be men obsessed by the Good News of
the kingdom and by a passionate desire to share that
News with others, then at least we would be men who
lived the model of the clerical life as set down by the
Council of Trent and by the various congregations of the
Roman Curia. Just as for the laity it was not necessary so

much to accept decisively and totally the Good News of the kingdom as it was to keep the commandments, so for us it was more necessary to say the breviary and avoid contact with women than to give ourselves over with delirious enthusiasm to proclaiming the presence of the kingdom and the dawning of the messianic age.

I am not angry, either at the institutional Church or at my seminary teachers. The style of evasion we practiced was centuries old; it may even contain somewhere deep within it some authentic insight. I am conscious that even now I am repeatedly trying to evade the challenge of the kingdom and the challenge of discipleship, so I cannot blame my predecessors for having developed a whole system of institutionalized evasions. We have not been much of a church down through the centuries. The point is that we are the only one there is, and even though we have fogged the message of Jesus and obscured the Good News of the kingdom, we are still the only community that exists for the purpose of proclaiming the kingdom and spreading the message. Anger at our failures is considerably less appropriate than understanding the reasons for the failures and resolving to do better.

But in the rigid structures of clerical culture, faith in the kingdom was not nearly so important as careful external conformity. It was not necessary that we be celebrants so long as we were obedient. We were not called upon to invite people to the wedding feast so much as we were expected to be on time for confessions on Saturday afternoons and evenings. As long as those structures were firmly maintained, we were not even aware of how shallow our convictions and how bland our enthusiasm really were. Nor did we understand that a life of celibacy can be painfully lonely if it is not somehow or other rooted in an experience of the fantastic Good News of that insanely generous and passionately loving God. It was not so much that we were not lonely but rather that our lives were so organized and routinized that we really did not have an opportunity to become aware of the fact of our loneliness.

The present crisis in the priesthood is, I think, based on the fact that the routines, the organizations, the structures, the props, and the masks have all been swept away, and we are being challenged to face our questions of conviction and commitment and to recognize our loneliness— a loneliness which for some personalities must be intolerable and which for many others can become meaningful and constructive and healthy only when the leap of existential commitment to the Good News has been made. I would not suggest that the problem for many priests (and for other, perhaps less official, disciples) is that they have "lost their faith" so much as it is that they have discovered their faith to be very inadequate and incomplete; that now for the first time in their lives they are being forced to face the challenge of the kingdom for what it really is. We know from historical precedent that men will try to evade the challenge of the proclamation of Jesus if they possibly can. It seems to me that the priesthood today, at least in the United States, is going through a difficult and painful period of recognizing Jesus' urgent call for decisive choice and trying to evade the stark fact that Jesus is demanding a response.

Some lay people have observed to me that from priests today one hears just about everything but proclamation of the Good News of the kingdom. One hears about race, about pollution, about war; one encounters priests who are counselors, community organizers, recreational supervisors, candidates for political office, T-group leaders, interior decorators, and even, on occasion (heaven protect us), sociologists. None of these roles prevent proclamation of the kingdom; all of them can be successfully integrated with the proclamation, but not a single one of them is an adequate substitute for issuing invitations to the wedding banquet. Many priests seem hesitant to commit themselves to the role of an eschatological herald because they are no longer sure that they believe in that role—another way of saying that they never really did believe in it. They do not think that such a role can be "relevant" in our "secularized" world, and they are not sure that people would take an eschatological herald seriously. The point is that to be really a disciple of Jesus one must be as committed to the message of the kingdom as he was, and to preach it whether or not the audience chooses to take it seriously or deem it relevant.

This book is not the appropriate place to discuss the "secularization" myth, but such an easily refuted sociological theory is embraced by many priests. The reason, it seems to me, is that it has proved a useful means of evading the challenge inherent in the New Testament. If Jesus is to be believed, if his message is to be taken seriously, if God indeed has intervened with loving and saving mercy, then the message is supremely relevant and the issuance of invitations to the wedding banquet is supremely important. But the fundamental issue is not whether men happen in the present time to deem the message relevant; it is whether it is a true message. This can be decided only by a leap of commitment. One cannot be a disciple without being committed, and if there are many hesitant disciples today, the reason is that they have not yet made an active commitment, perhaps even not yet had a full-fledged opportunity to choose for or against Jesus.

And make no mistake; that's what the issue is. The young cleric or nun who tells me that Jesus was a political revolutionary is not speaking either of the Jesus of the New Testament or of the Jesus of history as the New Testament scholars have discovered him. What they are speaking of is a Jesus created out of their own fantasy to help them evade the challenge of the New Testament. And when the young cleric or nun argues that he or she is not sure whether the New Testament is relevant anymore, they are

evading the real issue, which is whether the message of
Jesus is *true*. For if an eschatological age has dawned,
if God really was present in Jesus in a unique way, if we
are really privileged to be in intimate contact with the
Real on a basis of affectionate familiarity, then this Good
News is overwhelmingly relevant.

I do not reject the social concerns of the younger clergy
and the religious, though sometimes I wish they were rooted
in better informed and more sophisticated social analysis,
but I am saying that if these social concerns are not integrated with the self-definition as herald of an eschatological
banquet, as proclaimer of Good News, then the priest or
nun is simply not living the life of a disciple as Jesus
described it. They may be admirable and virtuous human
beings. They are not disciples of Jesus. As I have said in
previous chapters, for a Christian, personality growth and
social reform are a consequence of the fundamental commitment to the Good News of the kingdom, to good news
of God's fabulously generous love for us. Similarly, for one
who is a special herald of the kingdom, concern about
social injustice and human relationships is admirable, praiseworthy, even necessary; but as a consequence of one's
proclamation of the marriage feast and not as a substitute
for it.

If some of the clergy and religious do not want to proclaim the marriage feast, that is, of course, their privilege.
Vast numbers of people down through the ages haven't
proclaimed it. But if they will not proclaim it, they will
do themselves and us a great favor if they do not claim
to be disciples of Jesus and do not try to serve up to us
a Jesus that has nothing to do with the man we discover
in the New Testament.

Sometimes I allow myself to think that we may have
reached a turning point in the development of Christianity
in the Church and of the role of disciple of Jesus. We
know so much more now about the real meaning of the

New Testament. We also have far greater understanding of the workings of human societies and the development of human personalities. This new knowlege will make evasion much more difficult. The decision for or against the kingdom, a choice of either attending the marriage feast or not, will be much more difficult to evade in the years ahead.

But perhaps this hope of mine is foolish. We have shown remarkable ingenuity down through the centuries in coming up with new evasions when the old ones are stripped away. It may well be that extrinsic faith as a substitute for existential commitment is finished, but we may find ourselves a new substitute in the form of either radical social action or interpersonal aggressiveness masquerading as honesty. I am not so sure that I would like to choose between these two evasions; they are both singularly unattractive.

Most of those who are ex officio disciples have not lost the faith in the sense that they no longer believe at all in Jesus and his message, but many of them do not yet have the faith in the sense that faith means a definitive and total commitment to the Good News of the kingdom. The future of the Church in the United States, perhaps for centuries, depends on how many people in this present time of crisis are able to make such a leap. Or, to put it even more bluntly, how many will see that radical social action, be it of the romantic or intelligent variety, and interpersonal openness, be it of the sick or healthy variety, are not adequate substitutes for the proclamation of the Good News?

I have not watched the TV program "Laugh-In" for almost a year, but when I did there was an ongoing party inhabited by those bizarre "Laugh-In" characters. It never ended. Whenever the camera shifted, the party was rolling along with its characteristic frantic excitement. I often thought the "Laugh-In" party could easily be viewed as a secular symbol of the kingdom. For the wedding banquet to which we are invited is a party which never ends. Those of us who have decisively chosen for the Good News of Jesus are permanent participants of the banquet, and those who are called to be disciples of Jesus not only participate in the banquet but like Jesus venture forth to insist that those who have not responded to the invitation don't know what they are missing. But one can hardly renew an invitation to the banquet if one has never been inside.

CHAPTER 9

THE GAME PLAN

The prophet Isaiah was popular with the early Christian writers. Believing as they did that with the preaching of Jesus an eschatological age had begun, the Christian writers found a wealth of ideas and imagery in the writing of Isaiah. This was extremely helpful to them in recounting their experience of Jesus. Especially popular was the *Servant of Yahweh* poem in the fifty-third chapter of Isaiah. As C. H. Dodd points out in his pamphlet, *The Old Testament and the New,*[1] only one of the twelve verses of the poem is not quoted in whole or in part somewhere in the New Testament. Indeed, one sentence or other from the chapter is quoted, or at least alluded to, in all four gospels, in Acts, Romans, Philippians, Hebrews, and I Peter. Dodd notes that even if the original text of Isaiah had been lost it still would have been possible to reconstruct the servant song from allusions to it in the New Testament. In Chapters 8, 9, 10, Mark prepares the reader for the death of Jesus and clearly emphasizes that the sign to which Jesus would look would not be the sign of an apocalypse or a messianic military victory; it would be the sign of the Suffering Servant. Indeed, it is precisely the combination in these chapters of Mark of the apocalyptic Son of Man notion from Daniel with the Suffering

[1] C. H. Dodd, *The Old Testament and the New.* Facet Books, Biblical Series—3. Philadelphia: Fortress Press, 1963.

Servant notion from Isaiah which many writers take to be the core of the Christian insight. The eschatological age is not begun with marvels and wonders, much less with messianic victories. The Son of Man triumphs, rather, by becoming a Servant.

St. Luke begins his account of the public life of Jesus by relating the incident in the synagogue at Nazareth where Jesus applied to himself the passage from Isaiah 61:

> He came to Nazara, where he had been brought up, and went into the synagogue on the sabbath day as he usually did. He stood up to read, and they handed him the scroll of the prophet Isaiah. Unrolling the scroll he found the place where it is written:
>
> > *The spirit of the Lord has been given to me,*
> > *for he has anointed me.*
> > *He has sent me to bring the good news to the poor,*
> > *to proclaim liberty to captives*
> > *and to the blind new sight,*
> > *to set the downtrodden free,*
> > *to proclaim the Lord's year of favour.*
>
> He then rolled up the scroll, gave it back to the assistant and sat down. And all eyes in the synagogue were fixed on him. Then he began to speak to them, 'This text is being fulfilled today even as you listen'.[2]

John begins his gospel with a description of a wedding feast, an indication to most commentators that John is referring to the frequent Isaiahian theme of the new age, the messianic era, being a banquet. In other words, Jesus is the Suffering Servant of Isaiah who begins the era of the messianic banquet and who by his suffering brings glad

[2] Luke 4:16–22, *The Jerusalem Bible*. New York: Doubleday & Co., 1966.

tidings to the poor, liberty to captives, sight to the blind, and the release of prisoners—all as a sign of favor from Yahweh.

There is no doubt, then, that the New Testament writers thought of Jesus as beginning the messianic age as described by Isaiah, and interpreted Jesus' life and especially his death in terms of the Servant song from Isaiah. But an important question we must ask is whether Jesus used the Isaiahian imagery, particularly the Servant song, of himself. If he did, we have not only a perfectly valid interpretation of his life devised by the early Christians but also the interpretation Jesus chose for himself.

Here is the Servant song in its entirety:

"Who could believe what we have heard,
   and to whom has the power of Yahweh been revealed?"
Like a sapling he grew up in front of us,
like a root in arid ground.
Without beauty, without majesty (we saw him),
no looks to attract our eyes;
a thing despised and rejected by men,
a man of sorrows and familiar with suffering,
a man to make people screen their faces;
he was despised and we took no account of him.

And yet ours were the sufferings he bore,
ours the sorrows he carried.
But we, we thought of him as someone punished,
struck by God, and brought low.
Yet he was pierced through for our faults,
crushed for our sins.
On him lies a punishment that brings us peace,
and through his wounds we are healed.

We had all gone astray like sheep,
each taking his own way,
and Yahweh burdened him
with the sins of all of us.

Harshly dealt with, he bore it humbly,
he never opened his mouth,
like a lamb that is led to the slaughter-house,
like a sheep that is dumb before its shearers
never opening its mouth.

By force and by law he was taken;
would anyone plead his cause?
Yes, he was torn away from the land of the living;
for our faults struck down in death.
They gave him a grave with the wicked,
a tomb with the rich,
though he had done no wrong
and there had been no perjury in his mouth.

Yahweh has been pleased to crush him with suffering.
If he offers his life in atonement,
he shall see his heirs, he shall have a long life
and through him what Yahweh wishes will be done.

His soul's anguish over
he shall see the light and be content.
By his sufferings shall my servant justify many,
taking their faults on himself.

Hence I will grant whole hordes for his tribute,
he shall divide the spoil with the mighty,
for surrendering himself to death
and letting himself be taken for a sinner,
while he was bearing the faults of many
and praying all the time for sinners.[3]

Joachim Jeremias in his book, *The Central Message of the New Testament,* devotes ten pages to discussing the question of Jesus' interpretation of his own death. By careful textual analysis he first demonstrates that Jesus did indeed anticipate his death before it occurred. He also assures us (p. 45) that anyone who knows anything of the importance of the idea of the atoning power of suffering and death

[3] Isaiah 53, *The Jerusalem Bible, op. cit.*

in late Judaism will admit that it is "completely inconceivable that Jesus would have expected to suffer and die without having reflected on the meaning of these events."

Jeremias next carefully analyzes the five passages in the New Testament where Jesus applies the Servant song to himself. It is not our purpose here to engage in complicated exegetical debates, which are the proper field of the Scripture scholars, but let us quote one paragraph from Jeremias on what he considers to be the most important of the allusions to the Servant song, that found in the words of the institution of the Eucharist.

Among the texts in question, first of all attention must be drawn to the Eucharistic Words. What matters here are the words 'for many'. I will restrict myself to two remarks. In the first place, these words are preserved in all versions of the Words of Institution which the New Testament hands down to us, although with some variations as to position, and phrasing. Mark 14.24 says 'for many', Matt. 26.28 'on behalf of many', I Cor. 11.24 and Luke 22.19, 20 have 'for you', and finally John 6.51 writes 'for the life of the world'. Of the different versions of this expression, Mark's 'for many', being a Semitism, is older than Paul's and Luke's 'for you'. Since Paul is likely to have received his formulation of the Eucharistic Words in the beginning of the forties in Antioch, Mark's 'for many' leads us back into the first decade after Jesus' death. Whoever wishes to drop those two words as a secondary comment ought to realize that he is abandoning a very ancient piece of tradition and that there are no linguistic grounds on which he can stand. In the second place, the words 'for many' are a reference to Isa. 53, as Mark 10.45 confirms. The idea of substitution as well as the word 'many' alludes to just this passage, for 'many' without the article, in the inclusive sense of 'the many', 'the great number', 'all', abounds in Isa. 53 and constitutes something

like the keyword of this chapter. Thus, the phrase 'for
many' in the Eucharistic Words shows that Jesus found
the key to the meaning of his passion and death in Isa. 53.[4]

At the end of his analysis of the five passages, Jeremias
concludes that the primitive Christian interpretation of the
death of Jesus as a fulfillment of Isaiah 53, that is to say,
a suffering and death of service for many, can be traced
back to Jesus himself *with great probability*. He adds that
absolute certainty is not to be expected. One can be absolutely certain that the Servant song interpretation and
the related allusions to other passages in Isaiah date back
to the first few years, certainly well within the first decade,
after Jesus' death. In all likelihood, the Isaiah interpretation
goes back to Jesus himself.

It is, I think, legitimate for us to consider the Servant
theme to be at the very core of the message of Jesus. If
he did not use the words of Isaiah 53 himself, he acted
in such a way that almost immediately after his death his
followers virtually unanimously concluded that the Servant
song imagery was the best possible symbol they had to
describe what Jesus stood for.

But then what does it mean to say that Jesus was the
ebed-Yahweh?[5] The Servant is, first of all, the Servant of
Yahweh. He comes to do the will of his Father, even if
it means his suffering and death for "many."[6] He came
then, to serve Yahweh and to do His bidding. However
He bade Jesus also to serve others, to free them from cap-

[4] Joachim Jeremias, *The Central Message of the New Testament*. New
York: Charles Scribner's Sons, 1965, pp. 45–46.
[5] That word *ebed*, used in the Servant songs of Isaiah, is also used
in the synoptic gospels to describe the religious experience of Jesus
after his baptism. The voice of heaven is depicted as saying, "This is
my "servant" [*ebed*] in whom I am well pleased."
[6] It is well to note that in his original preaching Jesus did not expound
a complex theology of atonement such as is to be found in the later
books of the New Testament or in theological writing after the New
Testament era.

tivity, to help them to see, to walk, to hear, and to leap with joy. The primary service was to preach the Good News, to challenge the people to faith and then to encourage them to make the decisive act of responding to the challenge. It would be to read back into the first century our own more modern notions to think that "service" as it is used in the gospel means the kind of social action commitments which many Christians today try to justify as part of the *diakonia* of the Church. But the primary service of the *ebed-Yahweh* is service of Yahweh Himself. The secondary service is that of preaching the Good News of Yahweh's love.

However, the extension of this service to include a vast multitude of service activities to one's fellow man is certainly not invalid. The parable of the Good Samaritan, Jesus' compassion toward the poor, the sick, and the hungry, the warning that what is done to the least of the brothers is done to him, the insistence that the apostles serve one another as he had served him, all indicate that service is to be understood by the followers of Jesus as characteristic of all their relationships. But they must not forget that the primary service is owed to the heavenly Father. Other services are a consequence of that commitment. The heavenly Father has sent Jesus with the Good News for "the many." Jesus serves Him by preaching the Good News even to his death for "the many." The followers of Jesus are also to preach the Good News and thereby join in the service of Yahweh. But their commitment to the Good News and to its proclamation involves them necessarily and inevitably in lives of open, generous, serving love.

In effect Jesus said to his audiences, "A sign indeed you shall have, but it will not be the sign of the Romans being driven into the sea, nor a sign of the sun darkening; it will be a sign of the Servant of Yahweh, to be manifested first in my life and then in my death and also in the lives of my followers. Their joyous commitment to the Good

News of my heavenly Father's kingdom will be so powerful
that they will live lives of dedication and service that will
permit no doubt about the validity of my message. The
ultimate credentials I offer as spokesman for my Father in
heaven will be the kind of lives I and my followers after
me lived."

A perfectly splendid game plan I think we will all admit.
For if the followers of Jesus did indeed live the kind of
life he described, their witness would be irresistible. One
servant of Yahweh could easily be put down by the human
race (though as it turned out not permanently), but hundreds, thousands, millions of such servants would overwhelm the world. Human beings of the integrity, the
authenticity, the commitment, the generosity of Jesus, even
human beings who are pale imitations of Jesus, would
have been the most spectacular sign in the history of the
human race. A great game plan indeed, but as the pro-
football writers say, "it's a shame they didn't have the
personnel to execute it." For never in the long history
has there been more service than talk of it. By no means
have all those who claimed to be followers of Jesus been
servants in fact. They did not serve the little children as
Mark (9:30–37) interprets the story of the little children.
Nor do they imitate the meekness and humility of a child
in the sense of Matthew and Luke. Far too many popes,
bishops, priests, and laymen in the history of Christianity
have become arrogant, domineering tyrants more concerned with their own powers, privileges, and prerogatives
than with serving the people of God. Only he who is blind
and thinks the effectiveness of the Christian message depends on the perfection of churchmen will deny this fact.
Some of us have not been servants because we have been
proud and even ambitious men, but others of us, alas, have
refused to be servants from motives which have appeared
to be virtuous.

If we are to be servants, we must leave others free

to make their own religious decisions. We do not, however, wish to trust others with their freedom. We are afraid that, if they are free, they would make the wrong decisions, so we decide to reject the role of servant to assume the role of lord and ruler, not from ambition but from the desire that men and women be virtuous. We force them to do right *for their own good.* How much tyranny and oppression, how much lack of respect for the dignity and integrity of the individual person has masqueraded under those words?

But this is not the way of Jesus. He forces no one, he does not try to decide what people should do for their own good. He demands service and acts as a servant himself.

There is much contemporary criticism of ecclesiastical authorities for the pomp of their vestments and ceremonies, the ridiculously elevated titles with which they are addressed, and the isolated lives they live. I don't worry very much about any of these things. What a man is called or how he dresses or even where he lives are important only if he permits himself to think that titles and clothes and mansions make him somehow a superior man. I'm afraid the problem runs in the other direction. Ecclesiastical leadership has retreated behind titles, robes, and manions because it was afraid of service. Elaborate paraphernalia are an effect and not a cause; remove the cause and the effect is of peripheral importance. The cause, I suspect, is less that some ecclesiastical authorities are ambitious, though many of them truly are, but rather that many more of them are not really ready to trust their followers to make the right religious decisions. The servant role for such leadership is transformed into one of the imposition of virtue. It is an arduous and difficult role with few rewards and consolations. It may even be thought of as a form of service. But it is not the service of the New Testament; not the service of the invitation.

But why blame ecclesiastical leaders for a trait characteristic of all of us? Are parents really ready to be servants to their children, facilitating their offsprings' growth in the freedom to make their own decisions and to live their own lives? If parents are followers of Jesus of Nazareth, they must serve God by serving their children in the way Jesus served us. A parent not ready to respect his child's freedom of choice (appropriate, of course, to the age of the child) is scarcely in any position to be critical of ecclesiastical leadership which substitutes repression for invitation.

Service also ought to be characteristic of the relationship between husband and wife. The passage in Mark 10:2–16 about divorce is set in the context of Mark's development of the theme of the "cost of discipleship." Jesus is teaching that all who imitate his role as servant must approach even the marriage relationship with an attitude of service. Divorce is an easy escape from service to one's spouse, and it is rejected by Christians.

This passage from Mark has been so battered and beaten in attempts to use it to support now one side and now the other side of the debate on divorce that its whole striking emphasis is lost. It is worth while for us to consider it at some length, if only to get an idea about what Jesus meant by service.

It is necessary to remember that for the Jews adultery meant intercourse between a married woman and a man other than her husband. A woman could commit adultery against her husband and a man could commit adultery against another man, but a man could not commit adultery against his wife; that is to say, infidelity on the part of a male was not considered adultery in Jewish law. Thus, the teaching of Jesus in Verse 11 was strikingly novel, for it put husband and wife on a plane of complete equality. A man may no more put aside his wife than she can put him aside. It is this revolutionary attitude toward marriage that struck the apostles as being very harsh and making a fierce demand on their masculinity.

The prohibition of divorce in Mark 10:11 is absolute and is apparently both older and more authentic than the passage in Matthew which, at least in one text, seems to admit of an exception (Matthew 19:9). However, responsible Catholic scholars such as Alexander Jones are careful to point out that, while there is no doubt that Jesus is clearly laying down the ideal of Christian life, he is not specifying the exact marital legislation which would be appropriate for his followers in attempting to carry that ideal out in practice. It is extremely difficult to justify divorce in the face of its explicit proscription, but as Jones says, the passage must be interpreted "in the spirit," just as must all passages in the gospel. Thus, because Jesus leaves no question as to what the *ideal* of Christian marriage ought to be, this does not exclude the possibility of problems for those who through no fault of their own are not able to honor the ideal.

Jesus, however, was not attempting to provide information and quotations for the debate between Protestants and Catholics on divorce. He was, rather, speaking in the context of debates of his own time over the interpretation of Deuteronomy 24:1. The followers of Rabbi Shammai (who lived sometime before Jesus) were willing to permit divorce only on grounds of unchastity, whereas the disciples of Rabbi Hillel would permit divorce on much slighter grounds such as ugliness or even bad cooking. Jesus' statement of the ideal relationship between a man and a woman rejects the grounds of the debate.

Some Pharisees approached him and asked, 'Is it against the law for a man to divorce his wife?' They were testing him. He answered them, 'What did Moses command you?' 'Moses allowed us' they said 'to draw up a writ of dismissal and so to divorce.' Then Jesus said to them, 'It was because you were so unteachable that he wrote this commandment for you. But from the beginning of creation *God made them male and female. This is why a man must leave father and mother, and the two become one body.* They are no longer two, therefore, but one body. So then, what God has united, man must not divide.' Back in the house the disciples questioned him again about this, and he said to them, 'The man who divorces his wife and marries another is guilty of adultery against her. And if a woman divorces her husband and marries another she is guilty of adultery too.'

People were bringing little children to him, for him to touch them. The disciple turned them away, but when Jesus saw this he was indignant and said to them, 'Let the little children come to me, do not stop them; for it is to such as these that the kingdom of God belongs. I tell you solemnly, anyone who does not welcome the kingdom of God like a little child will never enter it.' Then he put his arms round them, laid his hands on them and gave them his blessing.[7]

Jesus shows here that the love between a husband and wife ought to be so strong and vigorous that there would be no thought of divorce between the two of them, that, indeed, the husband and the wife are equals. There is no more double standard by which a woman is held to moral requirements of which a man is free. In the next passage of Chapter 10 in Mark, Jesus shows that the openness and trust of little children, their docility, and their willingness to grow and to learn are to be other characteristics of his followers. It is not foreign to the context of these passages to link the two: only when husband and wife are willing to take on the style of little children in their relationship with one another, being as open and honest and trustful as

[7] Mark 10:2–16, *The Jerusalem Bible, op. cit.*

children are, can the ideal of Christian marriage be achieved.

Fear and suspicion are the two principal reasons for the decline of married love. We are afraid that if we permit our mate to know us as we really are, we will be ridiculed or taken advantage of. We are afraid that, if we open up to the other, we will lose our rights and be trampled upon. If we "give in" at all, we will never again be able to draw a line beyond which the other cannot come. We are suspicious of the other. He is a stranger, no matter how long we have lived together. We do not trust each other. We are not sure that he will be faithful and not desert us. We suspect that he will use our weakness and openness as an opportunity for cunning and selfishness, to cheat and make a fool of us. These emotions which cause us to harden our hearts in self-defense are part of the human condition. We use them to keep strangers, even friends, at bay. And in the most intimate relationship, that between a husband and wife, it is "natural" that we fall back on these defenses. But if it is natural, it is also disastrous, because these sorts of defenses make marital happiness impossible. It is precisely those defenses of fear and suspicion that Jesus asks us to give up if we are to be his followers.

The beginning of marriage is at its best a commitment to try to develop friendship—a commitment to begin a relationship of being servants to one another. But just as the whole Christian life is an experience of constantly growing in the skills of service, so must Christian marriage be an experience that never stops growing. Christian marriage is not a life that can be lived apart from the rest of the Christian mission. Only he who is willing to be a servant in marriage can be a servant beyond it, and only he who sees the servant theme as part of all of his life will have the courage, the bravery, the openness and trust to be a servant in marriage too.

We can get some idea how the early Church used the

implications in the Suffering Servant theme if we continue
to analyze Mark's gospel.

> James and John, the sons of Zebedee, approached him.
> 'Master,' they said to him 'we want you to do us a favour.'
> He said to them, 'What is it you want me to do for you?'
> They said to him, 'Allow us to sit one at your right hand
> and the other at your left in your glory'. 'You do not
> know what you are asking' Jesus said to them. 'Can you
> drink the cup that I must drink, or be baptised with the
> baptism with which I must be baptised?' They replied,
> 'We can'. Jesus said to them, 'The cup that I must drink
> you shall drink, and with the baptism with which I must
> be baptised you shall be baptised, but as for seats at my
> right hand or my left, these are not mine to grant; they
> belong to those to whom they have been allotted'.
>
> When the other ten heard this they began to feel indig-
> nant with James and John, so Jesus called them to him
> and said to them, 'You know that among the pagans their
> so-called rulers lord it over them, and their great men
> make their authority felt. This is not to happen among
> you. No, anyone who wants to become great among you
> must be your servant, and anyone who wants to be first
> among you must be slave to all. For the Son of Man himself
> did not come to be served but to serve, and to give his life
> as a ransom for many. (Mark 10:35–45)

In the passage preceding those quoted above, Jesus
makes his third and final prediction of the Passion. He is
explicit: he is going up to Jerusalem, he will be delivered
to the Gentiles, executed and on the third day he will rise.
Mark makes the point that Jesus deliberately set his face
toward Jerusalem, the known source of all his enemies, and
thereby consciously and freely accepts his messianic destiny.

Mark does not report the immediate reaction of the apostles to the prediction (as he does in Chapters 8:32 and 9:32 with the first two Passion presentiments). Instead, he relates the selfish request of James and John and the equally selfish response of the other disciples, which in the original tradition are probably unconnected. Thus Mark indicates that, once again, the disciples completely misunderstood Jesus' principal theme.

In his direct response to the sons of Zebedee Jesus makes two points: that positions of honor in God's kingdom are awarded in accordance with the decisions of a righteous God who could not be moved like some petty Oriental despot, and that in the days of his flesh their request lies completely outside Jesus' competence to fulfill.

He also points out that if there is to be any special place it will be for those who have rendered special service to others even to the extent of giving their lives through martyrdom.

The last paragraph of the above quoted passages appear in completely different contexts in both Luke and Matthew, indicating that they were part of collections of the sayings of Jesus which circulated without any particular context. Mark inserts them here because he finds them appropriate to his theme of Jesus as Suffering Servant and that the followers of Jesus be men committed to a life of service.

Mark ironically contrasts in these chapters Jesus' conception of his own role as Suffering and Ransoming Servant with the apostles' conception of his role as a political messiah. No matter how frequently he predicts his death, no matter how insistently he describes himself as a Suffering Servant, they simply will not understand. And in the midst of all his predictions, two of his followers manage to be so completely out of it that they are still worried about their own positions in the kingdom. Even as Jesus is on his way to Jerusalem to fulfill the will of the Father, his followers are engaging in trivial squabbles about their own prestige and status. It is easy for us to ridicule them for missing the point. However, haven't we missed the point too?

Jesus is asserting in this passage that his death is not an accident or a tragedy but an offering which is made freely and eagerly. He would give himself, and from this gift something of immense value would come. Every follower of Jesus must think of himself as freely, generously offering his life in the service of others. Our deaths ought not to be accidents or tragedies (though of course they will have an element of tragedy and perhaps accident, too). They should rather represent merely the conclusion of a life which has been from the beginning to end an exercise in gift-giving. But the question those who follow Jesus must ask themselves is, are we really giving life? Does our living bring ransom to any captives? Do our efforts bring release to any prisoners? Are we bringing hope and faith and love to very many people in the world around us, indeed, to anyone? We are called to give life; to give life to others by giving our own lives to them; to bring others hope and joy because of our hope and joy; to offer them faith because of the strength of our faith; to teach them how to love by the power of our love. If we live in such a way, then our death is as much an enthusiastic, conscious acceptance of God's will as the death of Christ. As we live, so we will die.

Mark concludes his tenth chapter with a final story to complete this extraordinarily brilliant theological reflection on the servant theme.

They reached Jericho; and as he left Jericho with his disciples and a large crowd, Bartimaeus (that is, the son of Timaeus), a blind begger, was sitting at the side of the road. When he heard that it was Jesus of Nazareth, he began to shout and to say, 'Son of David, Jesus, have pity on me! And many of them scolded him and told him to keep quiet, but he only shouted all the louder, 'Son of David, have pity on me'. Jesus stopped and said,

'Call him here'. So they called the blind man. 'Courage,' they said 'get up; he is calling you.' So throwing off his cloak, he jumped up and went to Jesus. Then Jesus spoke, 'What do you want me to do for you?' 'Rabbuni,' the blind man said to him 'Master, let me see again.' Jesus said to him, 'Go; your faith has saved you'. And immediately his sight returned and he followed him along the road. (Mark 10:46–52)

This passage acts as a transition between Jesus' Galilean ministry and his ministry in Jerusalem, and it concludes Mark's lengthy commentary on the need for followers of Jesus to imitate him as Suffering Servant, an imitation which Mark is urging on the early Christian converts.

The location of the miracle is important. Jesus is now drawing near to Jerusalem, Jericho being only fifteen miles away. It is his closeness to Jerusalem that justifies the end of Mark's "messianic secret." The fact that Jesus is the Messiah is no longer to be hidden for fear it will be misunderstood. All too soon he will demonstrate the precise nature of his messiahship—that of triumph through suffering and death rather than dazzling military victories. Jesus quite explicitly does not reprimand the blind man for proclaiming his faith in Jesus' messiahship. The passage is Mark's way of saying that now the lid is off.

Most authorities agree that the vivid details of the story indicate that it is being recounted by an eyewitness, though certainly its precise place in Mark's gospel is hardly accidental. The story contributes to the development of Mark's narrative and probably was part of the very early Christian catechesis even before the gospel was written, since it illustrates so precisely one of the important dimensions of discipleship—the need for enthusiastic faith.

Mark apparently intends us to contrast the enthusiasm and the faith of the blind man with the dullness of the apostles. The blind man does not have eyes and yet he really sees. The detail of Bartimaeus' throwing off his cloak indicates eagerness and enthusiasm, the promptness and spontaneity which are required of the man of faith. By leaping to his feet and dashing to Jesus he shows the enthusiasm that the apostles, who see but do not see, who follow but slowly and reluctantly, so sorely lack.

We of course wish to put ourselves on the side of Bartimaeus. We much prefer the blind man who saw and eagerly sought to follow Jesus. But in fact we probably have far more in common with the apostles. Bartimaeus knew what his problem was. How could one escape the obvious fact of physical blindness? He knew how utterly helpless he was unless the Messiah took pity on him. He knew that he could not exercise tight, unyielding control of his own life. He had to throw himself on the mercy of the Son of David. Our situation is as helpless as his. We, too, are utterly dependent on God's mercy, but we don't realize our dependence. We like to think that we are still in control of things. We like to think that we can impose our own carefully devised schedule on God's operations. Bartimaeus was blind and he knew it, so he could really see. Like the apostles, we are blind and do not know it, so we really cannot see. Jesus tries to open our eyes just as he tried to open the eyes of his apostles, but we obstinately refuse to open them because we are convinced that we already do see.

We also find ourselves embarrassed by Bartimaeus' headlong response. He dashes to Jesus, throwing off his mantle as he runs to him, and breathlessly pleads for his sight. He is a violently active man. He does not carefully fold his robe, neatly place it on the ground, and say to someone, "Look after this until I come back." He leaped and didn't look. We are cautious before jumping to our feet, and we are very careful about committing ourselves fully. Indeed, after carefully and cautiously evaluating the situation, we frequently do not leap at all. Jesus wants us to be headlong enthusiasts in our exercise of discipleship. When someone says to us about Jesus, "He is calling you," Jesus expects us to leap up and dash to him filled with throbbing, panting enthusiasm. It has been a very long time, I fear, since there was much throbbing, panting enthusiasm in most Christians.

Notice how the crowds try to throw a wet blanket on Bartimaeus' enthusiasm. They tell him to be quiet, not to bother Jesus with his request. They advise him that his enthusiastic faith and his eager commitment to the possibility that Jesus can cure him are foolishly optimistic. Who does he think he is that Jesus could possibly be concerned about him? Why should the Son of David, assuming that he is indeed the Son of David, possibly be concerned about a poor, ignorant blind begger? Forget your enthusiasm, Bartimaeus, he does not care about you. Shut up. Be quiet. Do not disturb the crowds. Do not upset the solemn occasion of the Master's trip to Jerusalem. Restrain your crude, foolish enthusiasm. That's what the wise men of the world tell the simple man of faith. But Bartimaeus is a tough customer. He does not quiet down. He does not take the advice of the wise men. He believes that the Son of David really can and does care about him, and so he keeps shouting. And what is the response to his enthusiasm? What is the response to his almost blasphemous belief that Jesus would care about him? The response is quick and simple: "Be on your way, your faith has saved you." And then what did Bartimaeus do after he received his sight? He began to follow Jesus on the road to Jerusalem. Maybe that's why we don't want to be enthusiastic about the possibility that Jesus really loves us; then we, too, would have to follow him on the road to Jerusalem.

We have quoted the tenth chapter of Mark and commented on it at considerable length because it is a splendid illustration of how even that first and most primitive of the

Christian gospels is in fact a brilliant, complex theological reflection, complete at the very end with a story of a blind man seeing just as the eschatological vision of Isaiah predicted that the blind would see in the messianic age. Bartimaeus' blindness is used as a symbol of the spiritual sight he already had but we lack. Jesus came that we might see, and the really important seeing is that by which we become conscious of the signs of the new eschatological age which has begun. Mark has used the tradition handed down to him as a means of instructing the early Christians on how they ought live in response to the invitation of Jesus.

The question of how much of the tenth chapter is a literal repetition of the words and deeds in the life of Jesus is academic. Mark was not trying to fool us, not trying to hide Jesus from us, not trying to distort his message. He was trying to explain to us, or rather to his immediate readers and through them to us, how he and the other early Christians experienced and understood the words and deeds of Jesus. And they experienced them as a profound call to service—a call which could be beautifully and brilliantly symbolized by allusions to the servant song of Isaiah. Jesus in fact was a Suffering Servant of Yahweh, even if he did not choose to call himself the Suffering Servant. Those who follow Jesus are also to serve Yahweh and, once committed to Him, are to lead lives of service to one another.

CHAPTER 10

MORE ABOUT BASIC THEMES

There are three other basic themes in the message of Jesus about which I think it is appropriate to comment: (1) universalism, (2) hunger, and (3) anger.

One of the most painful problems for modern Scripture scholars, as they try to penetrate beyond the layers of tradition to the original message of Jesus, is that the writers of the New Testament documents were dealing with very specific problems of their own. Mark, for example, was trying to explain to his readers why suffering was still necessary, why it was necessary for even Jesus to suffer when the messianic age had already begun. Luke was trying to explain why Jesus did not return though Jerusalem had fallen. Both writers also faced the need to exhort the early Christians who were often persecuted and discouraged. The rigorous canons which the Scripture scholars follow compel them to refuse the label "authentic" to any passage which cannot be clearly excluded from the literary concerns of the writers. Thus, if in a gospel we read of an incident in which Jesus apparently indicates that the Parousia will not occur in the near future, the scholars would say that it might very well be a literary device of the gospel author to cope with the problem of the delayed return of Jesus. Such a decision is, of course, not final, because other canons of criticism might restore the passage to the authentic category. Thus, if in the same incident Jesus is depicted as saying something unthinkable for the early Church to say, then the passage is more likely to be authenticated. So, when Jesus himself says that even he does not know when the Parousia will occur, the probability of that passage being authentic is enhanced. It must be remembered of course that "authentic" has for the critics a rather narrow meaning. It indicates that a given passage can be considered certainly, or at least with a high degree of probability, to be something that Jesus actually did or said and not a theological interpretation, reflection, or explanation of the early Church. If a passage is labeled "unauthentic" it does not indicate that the words or events did not happen; it means only that we cannot have a high level of confidence in it.

The problem of separating the theological and pedagogical concerns of the early Church from the actual events is especially difficult when one attempts to cope with the universalism of Jesus' message. By the time the gospels were written, the decisive choice had been made by the early Church to go beyond the synagogue into the Gentile world. Many of the Jewish Christians found themselves profoundly shocked by this decision, and, hence, all the gospel writers found themselves under severe constraints to justify what had been done. This does not mean that they distorted the tradition they received. But they eagerly searched for everything in the tradition which would have some bearing on the question of the universalism of the Good News.

Some scholars observe that the astonishing restraint of the gospel writers in the way they treated the traditional material they received is evidenced by their rigorous refusal to fabricate incidents in which Jesus visited Gentile countries or conversed with Gentile men and women. It would have marvelously suited their purposes to have provided a considerable number of stories of such events. Yet they recount only a few conversations and a couple of visits to Decapolis and to Phoenicia, which indicates that, however strong their controversial needs were, they simply did not feel at liberty to "doctor" the tradition. We can therefore assume that Jesus' healing of the daughter of the Syro-Phoenician woman does contain within it the core of a historically authentic trip. If one such story was made up, there was no reason why many more could not have been made up.

As we read through the gospels, we encounter many incidents in which the mission to the Gentiles is prefigured. For example, in the fourth chapter of St. Luke, Jesus is pictured as engaging in a rather bitter dialogue with his fellow citizens at Nazareth. He comments that a prophet should not expect honor in his own place. "Indeed, let me remind you there were many widows in Israel in the days of Elijah, when the heavens remained closed for over three years and a great famine spread over the land. It was to none of these that Elijah was sent, but to a widow of Zarephath near Sidon. Recall, too, the many lepers in Israel in the time of Elisha, yet none was cured except Naaman the Syrian." For such a sarcastic comment, Jesus was promptly thrown out of the synagogue.

The Scripture critics are at a loss when faced with a passage like that. How much of it actually represents a historical incident, and how much is Luke's theological reflection? The biting irony of Jesus' words gives at least some plausibility to the notion that they are too strong for his devoted followers to dare to put into his mouth.

But if it is difficult for us to say exactly how many of the references to the Gentiles found in the New Testament are considered to be historically authentic, it is not at all difficult to say that the message of Jesus was universalistic in its orientation. He may have spoken with few Gentiles and only occasionally traveled into Gentile land. He may not even have made many references in his preaching to them. The important point is that he preached the love of his heavenly Father—a love which transcended all boundaries,

Pharisee and publican, Jew and Samaritan, rich and poor, young and old. What is important in the Good News of Jesus is not who one is or where one comes from, but whether one responds to the invitation. Even if the Good News was announced in but one country originally and only to the members of one tribal group, it completely transcends the boundaries—political, religious, intellectual, and geographic—of that group. There were hints in Isaiah, of course, that the eschatological age would be for all men, and the Gentiles would beat a path to Zion. Apparently by the time of Jesus, Zion was thought to be some sort of political capital to which other tribes would come in respectful tribute. Just as the message of Jesus rejected completely the notion of a political messiah, so it also rejected the idea of an Israelite empire. The kingdom to be centered in Zion would be a kingdom of those who responded to the invitation of the heavenly Father to call him "Father dear" and to enter into his splendid wedding festival. The resistance of many of the Jewish Christians to following the implications of that message to its logical conclusion is understandable, as was, indeed, the resistance of the citizens of Nazareth. It was bad enough that God loved them, it was even worse that God loved all men. We are not at all sure that we want to accept the Good News, but it is even worse if we are faced with the annoying fact that we must share it with others. In fact, if part of the Good News is that God loves everyone, we begin to rather doubt that it is *Good* News. We don't want to believe in God's love when it is directed just at us, but when it is directed at everyone else it seems much better not to believe in that love at all.

When we describe the response to Jesus in such a fashion, the absurdity of the reaction seems obvious. Yet the citizens of Nazareth had no monopoly on it. It is as difficult for us today to accept the universality of God's love as it was for them. If Jesus came into our town and announced that God loved the Chinese, the North Vietnamese, and the Russians every bit as much as he loved us, he would run a serious risk of being pushed over a cliff once again.

And if he should attend a meeting of the most radical or liberal Catholic enthusiasts and tell them that his heavenly Father loved the white ethnic racists and the polluters of the environment and even the fat cats of the Establishment, he would be very lucky to get out of that meeting without having obscenities hurled at him.

We have, of course, made some progress since the time of Jesus. We now love some others not part of our own racial, religious, or ethnic group. It is now fashionable in certain circles to love blacks, particularly when they are of the militant or violent variety, young people, particularly if they are drug addicts, and poor people, especially if they march on picket lines. But it is hardly expected of us to love hardhats, or middle-class Americans, or suburban executives, or Republicans, or squares. Fashions change of course. The ethnic hardhats thirty years ago were the "working masses." Professor Michael Lerner tells us of his colleague at Yale who when he heard that Italian candidates were daring to challenge Mayor Lindsay for that unenviable role commented, "If there is one inferior people in the country, I am convinced it must be the Italians."

The reader may suspect by now that I am more than a little fed up with the snobbery, the faddism, and the selective compassion of academia. Not all academics behave that way, of course. The point is, however, that even in the most enlightened and sophisticated segments of what is supposedly a progressive and intelligent society bigotry is still very much with us. It did not go out of fashion when Jesus passed through the crowd at Nazareth and shook the dust of that obscure little hamlet from his feet. Selective compassion, the lionizing of one group (so long as it acts according to our prescribed expectations), has absolutely nothing to do with the message of Jesus of Nazareth. Jesus tells the university professor that he must love the Polish hardhat and even try to see the world from his perspective in order to understand sympathetically the other's position. He tells the white racist that he must strive to understand the reasons that lie behind the black man's militancy, and he tells the black militant that he must make every effort to understand and even sympathize with the fear of the racist. He tells the old that they must not write off even the most repulsive inhabitants of the youth culture, and he warns the youth culture that the generation gap is not a virtue but a barrier. Scapegoating, no matter how popular and pervasive a human activity, is not permitted to the follower of Jesus. The only men legitimately villains are ourselves, and the only villainy is that of refusing to accept the invitation to the kingdom.

This is a hard saying. Hatred is so marvelously useful to mobilize human emotions, to give movements their energy and drive, to force causes toward fulfillment and victory. We do not want our movements and our causes to be fundamentally rooted in hatred, but we do use "just a little bit" to be sure that the energies and enthusiasms of our colleagues do not lag. Only there is no such thing as "a little bit of hatred," and any cause which allows itself to be infiltrated by it will ultimately be destroyed by it.

And yet we profoundly suspect those who are different from us. The Hindus fight the Moslems in India; the Malays and the Chinese struggle in Singapore; the East Indians and the natives eye one another with suspicion in the Fiji Islands; black and white war with each other in South Africa, and black and brown in the Caribbean islands; English and Welsh and Scots revive old animosities in Great Britain; and the last battles of ecumenism will surely be waged in the streets of Belfast and the plains of Derry. The Ibos fight the Hausas to the death in Nigeria; the Chinese and Russians spar with one another along the two-thousand-mile border; in Canada the conflict between British and French grows more serious; and across the English

Channel, even after the departure of Le Général, one frequently doubts that the Hundred Years' War ever ended. As Jesus of Nazareth contemplates this fantastic array of hatred, he must say to himself, "I don't think they yet understand what I was talking about."

There is an incredible amount of diversity in the world. Some of us are tall, some short; some fat, some thin; some of us have straight hair, some of us have kinky hair; some have thin noses, some wide; some brown skin, others white, yellow, and everything in between; some of us enjoy sexual attractiveness to a voluptuous extreme and others display a more austere, restrained sexuality (not necessarily less powerful). Such diversity is one of God's jokes, it seems to me. He could have made the human race in a much more standardized form. But as in so many other things, he outdid Himself. He produced a staggering amount of diversity, which probably vastly amuses Him. He undoubtedly wonders and is disappointed that we do not get the joke. For instead of enjoying the diversity of the race, we have used it as an occasion for conflict and hatred. Wars have been fought over skin color, hair length, eating habits, languages, and almost every other conceivable difference. Amazingly enough, sometimes these differences are not distinguishable to those not party to the conflict. Most Americans, I dare say, would be hard put to distinguish between a Biafran and a Nigerian. And most Nigerians would not think an English Canadian was at all different from a French Canadian. Even the faintest of differences can mean not just that we notice the difference but that we feel the other is inferior and may be plotting against us; therefore we must destroy him before he destroys us.

No, the citizens of Nazareth were not the last ethnocentrics.

And the point of Jesus' message is as pertinent today as it ever was: unless we believe in the heavenly Father (or a Really Real), who does in fact love all of us to a point of insane generosity, we human beings are simply incapable of being generous in our love of others. We may honor such universality of love and compassion in theory, but in practice we end up with our scapegoats and our villains, with our "good guys" and our "bad guys," with those whom we feel constrained to love and those whom we feel perfectly free to hate. What a pathetic character man is. He has an immense capacity for love, but a great fear of what it will do to him; so he defends himself against its demands by retreating behind the barriers of hatred. Jesus of Nazareth says, "If you believe that my heavenly Father loves you, if you believe that the universe is out to do you good, then you know you have nothing to fear; you do not run so very great a risk by putting aside the defenses of hatred and permitting yourself to make that terrifying leap of faith which is called love."

Who knows, you may even be able to love the Samaritans.

One of the more astonishing aspects of the person of Jesus, at least to me, is his capacity for anger. The meek and mild Jesus of the nineteenth- and early twentieth-century biographies is simply not to be found in the New Testament. He is a man who speaks his mind, even at the risk of offending others. He vigorously denounces hypocrisy and injustice, and angrily excoriates those who impose foolish religious burdens. And while he is patient with the weakness and frailties of his disciples, he never permits them to deceive themselves as to what he thinks of their foolishness. His "Get thee behind me, Satan" statement to Peter (most likely an authentic logion, because the early Church would scarcely present Peter in such an unfavorable light) comes from a man not at all hesitant to give vent to the emotion of anger.

The humanist psychologists, such as Abraham Maslow, insist that the capacity to love and the capacity to be angry are closely related; that we can only be free to love when we can be free to be angry. The man who tries to love while restraining his anger is apt to become a passive-aggressive personality. He uses his love as a means of controlling and manipulating others as he is unable to experience anger in his relationships with them.

For some strange historical quirk, which I do not fully understand, popular piety has insisted on portraying Jesus as a passive-aggressive person, one who meekly and patiently loved and only rarely expressed the opposite side of passion, anger. And the model of the Christian life urged on so many of us in seminary and novitiate days was the model of the passive-aggressive person or "the nice guy." Not only were we not permitted to express our anger, we were urged to pretend we didn't have it. We were told that the meek would possess the earth. They never told us that the word "meek" in the Beatitudes actually means "one who is humble and open-minded to the inspiration of God's spirit." The only sort of anger we thought could exist was that of blind fury, and of course that was generally the kind of anger we experienced; it devastated others like a hurricane.

When I speak of anger, however, what I really mean is the capacity to assert our own dignity and our own integrity and our own reality in our relationships. It is the ability to be ourselves even when that offers a challenging demand to our role opposite in a relationship. The angry man understands that an expression of his own selfhood in a relationship may cause some suffering, but he realizes that less suffering is involved in the long run than if he were to restrain his anger, hide his selfhood, and pretends to a peace and tranquillity that do not in fact exist. One presumes that Jesus knew he would hurt Peter when he called him Satan and told him to get behind him. He certainly understood that it might hurt his mother when he indicated to her that her time would come only after his death, and surely he realized that James and John would be offended when he abruptly rejected their claim for priority in the kingdom. But he did not compromise, he did not equivocate, he did not evade; he bluntly and firmly asserted his own selfhood.

I suppose I am particularly impressed by this phenomenon because one of the major defects of my own personality is my inability to express anger. I can do it (perhaps all too well) in the written word, but in face-to-face relationships, I find myself almost compelled to shy away from the possibility of causing pain to someone else. It would be easy to scapegoat my seminary training (blaming the seminary is one of the great indoor sports of the clergy today), but I am aware that this problem goes far back beyond seminary days. I am getting somewhat better at it, at least in certain relationships, and I am not "a nice guy" who attempts to manipulate others by serving them. On the contrary, I am more inclined to express my anger by assuming the martyr's role in my relationships with others. However, the step from a long-suffering, patient, sainted martyr to a raving, ranting man possessed by a towering rage is all too short.

And it is a step that is frequently taken at the wrong time. Any unfortunate who happens to cross my path at the wrong moment is likely to be the victim of a rage long building up.

I remember one particularly disgraceful incident when I was presiding over what was, alas, the largest teen club on the South Side of Chicago. It had been a bad night. I was being harassed by a pastor, a mother superior, a janitor, a parents' committee, an irresponsible hi-club president, a dizzy female vice-president, a couple of thieves, beer drinkers, an incredibly incompetent policeman, and a number of ingenious characters who thought that the great challenge of the evening was to find a way to avoid paying the twenty-five-cent admission fee. About ten-thirty, two young men who were among my closest friends and co-workers in the parish arrived on the scene two hours later than they should have. One of them jokingly remarked, "You really don't expect us to pay our twenty-five cents now, do you?" After the first three seconds of my tirade, they fled in terror.

Half an hour later I found them to apologize. But I think to this day they don't quite understand what happened.

I become autobiographical at this point because I suspect that in this matter I am typical of countless Catholics. We hold our anger back, being afraid of vigorously and forcefully asserting ourselves in human relationships for both personality and religious reasons. If the result is not an occasional towering rage, then it is something worse, a subtle but pervasive punishment of others under the guise of love. Of the two, I think the towering rage is preferable.

But whichever choice we make, it ought to be perfectly clear that it cannot be justified in the person or the word or the deed of Jesus of Nazareth. He allowed himself to be led to the cross, indeed, like a lamb to the slaughter; he almost exulted in his own weakness and frailty. But at no point did he stop being himself. We need to read only the account of his trial to realize that this was not a passive-aggressive man. He was not afraid to be angry, but neither did he need to be angry. It is almost as though the presence or absence of anger was no great problem for him. He was conscious of his mission: he had come to proclaim the kingdom of his Father and to invite everyone to share in the festivities of that kingdom. He would tolerate no perversions of the message of the kingdom, and when anyone attempted to pervert it, his reaction was quick and powerful. Even his closest and most adoring follower heard the terrible words, "Get thee behind me, Satan."

Finally, when one reads the New Testament, one cannot escape the impression that there is an immense amount of talk about food. There are wedding banquets, miraculous meals in the desert, descriptions of people hungering and thirsting after righteousness, the assertion by Jesus that he is the Bread of Life, the Last Supper with the apostles. The emphasis shifts back and forth from the real to the symbolical. Jesus' compassion for the crowd because they were hungry is both a sympathy for their physical hunger in the desert and, perhaps more, a sympathy that they do not even realize how hungry they are for the Bread of Life. And in the sixth chapter of St. John, the alternating emphasis on Jesus as Wisdom and Jesus as Eucharist reduces such a skillful, clear writer as Father Raymond Brown to using diagrams. But the important hunger is, of course, the eschatological hunger, the hunger for the fullness of God's kingdom, the hunger for the completion of the love which Jesus has come to announce.

And yet the meals described in the New Testament are by no means simply symbols. The wedding feast at Cana and the Last Supper, for example, are real assemblies of real people with real hopes and real fears. Some Scripture authorities even suspect that the Last Supper was not by any means the first supper, and that the meals that Jesus had with his disciples throughout his public ministry were not just functional events but at least some of them took on the significance of a religious banquet, a simultaneous and foreshadowing of the banquet in the kingdom of the heavenly Father. The Last Supper and the Eucharistic celebrations after the resurrection were a continuation of a religious custom already being celebrated during the active ministry of Jesus.

Eating is such a basic and primal human activity that, like that other basic and primal activity, sexuality, it almost inevitably takes on religious symbolism. It represents man's basic union with the physical forces of the universe and also his communion with others with whom he shares this vital human activity. We are hungry for the banquet in the kingdom of God not merely as individuals but as members of a community. The fact that eating is a communal activity almost demands that those who share in the meal which foreshadows the fullness of the messianic banquet be themselves a community. Even if we had no other evidence that the message of Jesus necessarily led to the emergence of a community of Christians, the symbolism of the messianic banquet and the fact of the communal meal of Jesus and his followers would certainly indicate that even during the public life of Jesus a church was slowly coming into being.

Hunger, in the final analysis, stands for human loneliness, the desperate longing of man for union. When we eat we take the physical world into our bodies in order to assuage our physical hunger. But man also has a capacity for the infinite, a hunger for everything, a longing for the absolute. When Jesus proclaimed himself the Bread of Life, that he came to offer man food after which they would never hunger and drink after which they would never thirst, he was asserting that the Good News of his heavenly Father's kingdom was a response to man's yearning for the Infinite, his hunger for the Absolute. It was just one more part of the Good News that was too good to be true.

CHAPTER 11
HE LIVES

After a fairly long period when Catholic theology paid little attention to it, the resurrection is once again on center stage among Catholic concerns, and that is, of course, where it ought to be, because it is impossible even to imagine the existence of Christianity in the absence of the Easter phenomenon.

My own personal hunch is that the resurrection issue will become more and more important as the years go on. The human race has discovered that man is never too old to grow and that personality growth and development come through a process of death and resurrection; the experience of putting off the fears and protections of one's defensive armor plate in opening oneself to a new life. St. Paul's description of putting off the old man and putting on the new turns out to have been rooted in a very sound psychological insight. Experiencing resurrection is a constant dimension of life, a resurrection preceded by and made possible through a death. Modern man will, I think, shortly have to ask himself which of these two intimately related realities is the ultimate one.

But if the resurrection is center stage in Catholic thought, it does not follow that the discussion of it is always helpful.

There are in Catholic circles, it seems to me, four "fallacies" which seem to focus on the Easter phenomenon:

1. Emphasis on the resurrection which ignores the cross.
2. Emphasis on the individual resurrection which ignores the communal nature of New Life.
3. Emphasis on the facts of the resurrection narratives without much attention paid to the meaning of the Easter event.
4. Emphasis to a point almost of compulsiveness on future personal resurrection while isolating this from the rest of the message of the kingdom.

In his book, *Jesus Means Freedom*, Ernst Käsemann devotes a brilliant chapter to the discussion of Paul's dealing with the resurrection issue in his epistle to the Corinthians. Käsemann shows how the disorder and enthusiasm of the Corinthian was founded on the misunderstanding of the nature of the resurrection. The Corinthians thought that the battle was all over, that the resurrection had already occurred, and that all they had to do was enjoy its fruits.

> Anyone who feels himself to be a citizen of heaven and permeated with heavenly strength no longer needs to take the earth seriously. He has all the less need to do so if he has already been drawn into the largely orgiastic doings of the mystery religions, and is accustomed in his proletarian existence to accident and uncertainty, so that one must not assume that his old Adam is strictly regulated. Exuberant religious vitality breaks through every dyke and stops for no bourgeois taboo.[1]

In such a view of the resurrection, then, the cross was completely forgotten. Oh, it may have been an action which preceded the resurrection, but it had no particular meaning

[1] Käsemann, Ernst, *Jesus Means Freedom*. Philadelphia: Fortress Press, 1968, p. 64.

for the present situation in which men found themselves. The lid was off; the sky was the limit.

> Why should the woman keep silence when the Spirit has come upon her? Why should the slave consent to be dependent on a Christian master? Why should not prophets and those who speak in tongues speak as often as they wish, if they are inspired? Why should one not on the one hand practice asceticism to show that his state is like that of the angels, and on the other hand cohabit with his stepmother to show that Christ has freed us from the moral prejudices of a bourgeois world? Freedom has become the real and the sole mark of the Christian and the church. Do we not renounce all the bliss that has been bestowed on us, if we do not turn it to account incessantly and in relation to everyone?[2]

It is perhaps no accident that similar enthusiasms can be found today in certain Catholic quarters. The emphasis on resurrection in the theology from the last decade has removed the cross from many people's minds and produced displays of emotional orgies not unlike that on which Paul had to depend at Corinth. My colleague, Father Raymond Brown, at the International Conference in Brussels in 1970 insisted that the two events could not be separated (much to the offense of some of the amateur theologians in the crowd). Käsemann makes exactly the same point:

> . . . for Paul he remains the Crucified One. That is not meant historically, so that the cross is the way to exaltation, although that naturally was the case. It is meant, rather, that Christ, exalted above the cross in his sublimity, is misunderstood if one separates the exaltation from the

[2] *Ibid.*, p. 64.

cross, and so reduces their relationship to that of two merely consecutive events. The Risen and Exalted One remains the Crucified One; and his sovereignty is not understood and acknowledged if the cross is merely made the last station on his earthly way. . . .[3]

For the battle is not yet over. The sovereignty of Christ is still being disputed by the power of death. The kingdom is not yet fully come. The message of the Good News has not yet been accepted. Even the vindication of Jesus in the resurrection event has not enticed everyone to the wedding feast and therefore the service of the Suffering Servant of Yahweh must continue at least in his church. The resurrection for us is still a promise of the future. As Käsemann notes, "What ultimately matters is not that we genuinely believe and defend this preaching, but that we accept it as a call to walk as Jesus' disciples and to share his death."[4]

Käsemann adds later:

A man counts as a lover of the cross only in so far as it enables him to come to terms rather with himself and others and with the powers and enticements of the world. Under the cross man attains manhood, because that is where God reveals himself as what he really is—our Creator. . . .
[p. 76]
Christ's victory begins in our hearts. That does not eliminate the evil forces that surround us; but if the spell is broken in our heart the good effects spread indefinitely. The church that is worthy of the name is a band of people in which the love of God has broken the spell of demons and strange gods and is now pushing its way into the world.[5]

[3] *Ibid.*, p. 67.
[4] *Ibid.*, p. 75.
[5] *Ibid.*, pp. 76–77.

The resurrection, then, began with Jesus, but with us it is yet to come. Our lives are still lives of suffering service. We still walk the way of the cross.

> Anyone knowing merely the risen Lord who has left his cross behind is no longer speaking of Jesus of Nazareth, and so his theology of resurrection can leave us cold. For no theory of the resurrection that does not become a theology of the cross is bound to lead, as the Corinthian example shows, to a wrong-headed enthusiasm . . . there is no sharing in the glory of the risen Lord except in the discipleship of the cross.[6]

One wonders even that it is necessary to say this. Even if the New Testament was not clear on this, we need merely to look at our own lives and recognize how painful the experience of service is to understand that the kingdom is not yet completely come, that the wedding feast has only begun, and that the resurrection exists rather in down payment than in reality. Joy we may have, but surely not yet the fullness of joy. Nevertheless, the intimate relationship between cross and resurrection seems to have been repeatedly misunderstood down through the history of Christianity. The enthusiasts of Corinth were not the last of their breed.

Exultation came to Jesus through service—painful, difficult service—and there is no other option available to us. The enthusiasts who attempt to eliminate the cross from Christianity or attempt to short-circuit the process or to simplify it to an "encounter" session use a massive denial mechanism, a mechanism which at root confuses the euphoria of hope and enthusiasm with faith—and, incidentally, also frequently confuses aggressiveness and hard sell with charity. Suffering service described in the tenth chapter of St. Mark is still

[6] *Ibid.*, p. 82.

the game plan. It is service, of course, mixed with joy. We already are at a wedding banquet, but it is only beginning. The main course has not yet been served.

If "resurrection without the cross" is a theory that has once again emerged in the Catholic community, the idea of a purely individual resurrection has been with us for a long time. In a rather pedantic article in the Scripture issue of *Concilium*, 1971, Joseph Blenkinsopp ridiculed the idea of the immortality of the individual soul and the resurrection of the individual body separate from a renewed life for the whole of creation. There isn't much doubt that the separated soul is a concept quite foreign to the New Testament. Furthermore, there is also evidence that Jesus came to preach a whole new creation in which life was promised not merely to individuals but to the whole race and, indeed, to the whole material world, which as St. Paul observes is groaning for redemption. Blenkinsopp is perhaps too harsh on the popular piety, because, while its symbols (like all symbols) are inadequate, they did represent a conviction about life which was basically sound. We cannot separate our own destinies from the destiny of the race, and we cannot separate mankind's destiny from that of the universe. The individual of course does live, but he does not live alone. He will find everlasting life only as a part of the human community, only as an element in the whole of creation. The heavenly Father's love, which Jesus announces, is a love for the whole of creation manifested in and through man and permeating to the very outer limits of the universe. *Everything* is to be restored in Christ, and the religious inner-directed man working out his own personal salvation and resurrection by himself has missed an extremely important point in the teaching of Jesus.

But it seems to me that the most serious misplaced emphasis, one that has been with us persistently almost from the beginning of Christianity, is that which argues interminably over the details of the resurrection and ignores its meaning.

I once sat in on a conversation of very learned theologians in which an argument raged over whether a TV camera at the entrance of the tomb on Easter morning would have recorded anything at all. I must confess that my sense of the absurd got the better of me, for I imagined not just the TV camera but Walter Cronkite or perhaps Howard Cosell and Dandy Meredith commenting on the event. (Indeed, I even thought of Dandy saying, "It sure is good to have ole Jesus back with us again!") I should have thought that the important point is that Jesus lives; that the way the heavenly Father vindicated him in the face of his enemies was considerably less important than the *fact* that the vindication did occur.

I would be quite content to leave the methods by which the Father accomplished the vindication to His own choosing. Incidentally, one must say from purely objective grounds that the vindication has been successful. Those who accused and then executed Jesus thought they would get rid of him, that he would be removed from the public scene and no one would ever hear of him again. They were quite confident that Jesus' days of troublemaking were over. The historical record shows how wrong they were, and even if one rejects completely any new life for Jesus after his death, he still must admit that he won and his enemies lost. They are forgotten, but Jesus and his troublemaking go merrily on.

Gunther Bornkamm makes an extremely useful distinction between the message of the resurrection and the historical problems of the narrative. The message is totally single in its content and import, but the narratives are filled with ambiguities.

The event of Christ's resurrection from the dead, his life and his eternal reign, are things removed from historical scholarship. History cannot ascertain and establish conclusively the facts about them as it can with other events of the past. The last historical fact available to them is the Easter faith of the first disciples. What the message and the experience on which it was founded mean is not hidden by the New Testament. This belief is not the particular experience of a few enthusiasts or a particular theological opinion of a few apostles, which in the course of time was fortunate enough to establish itself and make a big success. No; wherever there were early Christian witnesses and communities, and however varied their message and theology were, they are all united in believing and acknowledging the risen Lord. . . .

At the same time, just as certainly as—even in a completely historical sense—there would be no gospel, not one account, no letter in the New Testament, no faith, no Church, no worship, no prayer in Christendom to this day without the message of the resurrection of Christ, even so difficult and indeed impossible is it to gain a satisfactory idea of how the Easter events took place. There is an undeniable tension between the singleness of the Easter message and the ambiguity and historical problems of the Easter *narratives*. We cannot deal with this in all its detail here.[7]

So what we do, of course, is concentrate on the ambiguity of the narratives and ignore the message. It is really much easier to do this, because if we can lose ourselves in the conflicting details of the narratives, we do not have to face the facts of the message—that is to say, the fact that the Father vindicated Jesus even as Jesus promised that He would. It is so very easy both for theology and apologetics to simply become highly sophisticated forms of evasion.

The Dutch Catholic Scripture scholar, Bas van Iersel, in an article in the 1971 Scripture issue of *Concilium*, asks whether the resurrection narratives in the New Testament are intended to be information or interpretation. Are they

---

[7] Bornkamm, *op. cit.*, pp. 180–81.

primarily historical accounts purporting to describe exactly
how things happened, or are they interpretation, that is to
say, do they attempt to assign a meaning to the resurrection
phenomena without informing us specifically about events.
Van Iersel concludes that only Luke 24:36–43 can be identi-
fied as traditional with "sufficient probability."

> This particular traditional matter here seems to show
> a risen person, tangible, observable, not only with flesh
> and bones but actually eating in view of all present, and
> so identifying himself as Jesus. This observation of Jesus
> does not seem to presuppose faith. On the contrary, the
> whole passage gives the impression that perplexity, be-
> wilderment, fear, doubt and even disbelief can be over-
> come by sensual seeing and touching. It seems wholly
> justified to bring up this tradition as an argument against
> the assertion that the risen Lord holds himself aloof from
> observation and any perception which occurs outside the
> faith. In any case this text should serve as a warning to
> us not to sever the risen Christ from the tangible Jesus.[8]

Yet van Iersel says that even this passage is more interpretation than information, that it is "polemical and directed against the docetic opinion which began to emerge";
that is to say, it was an argument against those who deny
that Jesus was a real man rather than a strictly historical
narrative.

But if van Iersel thinks that the resurrection narratives
are more likely interpretations than information, it is "a way
of interpreting handed over to the original community" and,
indeed, handed over to it quite independently of the general
Jewish expectation of the resurrection of the dead. Van

[8] Bas van Iersel, "The Resurrection of Jesus—Information or Interpretation," trans. by Theo Westow, *The New Concilium: Immortality and
Resurrection*. New York: Herder and Herder, pp. 65–66.

Iersel concludes: "I would therefore say that this way of interpreting is also derived from the facts. But about the nature of these facts and their verifiability we are wholly in the dark."[9]

Bornkamm observes that we must view the Easter stories as evidence of faith and not as records of chronicles, and we must seek the *message* of Easter when we read the stories and not a literal description of Easter.

Comments like these cause profound scandal to some Christians as though somehow or other their faith in the resurrection is based on the New Testament's providing a videotape replay of the event. In that case we have a historically validated fact and we do not need faith. That George Washington defeated the Hessians at Trenton is not an object of faith at all. It is something we can confirm by historical scholarship. But the fact of the resurrection can never be confirmed by historical fact. Even if the narratives we have were literal descriptions of certain events, it would still require a leap of faith to interpret these events as actually meaning that a man had risen from the dead; and much more—that all of us were to rise from the dead. The question is not, do we have an accurate picture of the facts of Easter, but do we believe in Easter? All the facts in the world do not make that leap of faith one bit easier. The message is far more important than facts (though of course the message presupposes some facts). The critical question for us is the message.

We can be quite certain of some facts. The early Christians had a profound experience of Jesus immediately after his death. In Bornkamm's words, "What became clear and grew to a certainty for the Church was this, that God himself intervened with his almighty hand in the wicked and rebellious life of the world, and had wrestled this Jesus of Nazareth from the power of sin and death which had risen against him, and set him up as Lord of the world."[10] This

[9] *Ibid.*, p. 66.
[10] Bornkamm, *op. cit.*, p. 83.

was the way people felt shortly after Jesus' death. They experienced Jesus as vindicated even as he foretold he would be. The experience for them was one of faith, as it is for us today, but that the experience occurred is a historical fact. It cannot be written off as a plot, a conspiracy, or a slowly developing evolutionary process. Immediately after his death there was a fantastic experience of him as alive. Jesus' own message of the coming of the kingdom was preached once again, but now he himself, together with his death and resurrection, in Bornkamm's words, "has entered into this message and become the core of it."[11]

How we choose to cope with this experience, whether we accept the interpretation put on it by the early Christians and embodied in the resurrection narratives we have, is ultimately dependent on our faith. But the experience itself is indisputable. Was it a monstrous delusion or is it true that God has acknowledged Jesus, whom the world refused to acknowledge? Was there really an event that took place in this time and in this world even though it puts an end and limit to this time and to this world? That is the issue that must be faced and it will never be faced as long as we quibble about the details of the resurrection narrative.

Bornkamm insists that if we are to face the issue we must look squarely at the contrast between what men did and do and what God has done and accomplished in and through Jesus as this contrast is manifested in the New Testament interpretations of the resurrection. Bornkamm then demonstrates with considerable skill how these two narratives interpret God's vindication of Jesus and the resurrection event.

The men and women who encounter the risen Christ in the Easter stories, have come to an end of their wisdom. They are alarmed and disturbed by his death, mourners wandering about the grave of their Lord in their helpless love, and trying like the women at the grave with piti-

11 *Ibid.*, p. 184.

able means to stay the process and odour of corruption, disciples huddled fearfully together like animals in a thunderstorm (Jn. xx. 19ff.). So it is, too, with the two disciples on the way to Emmaus on the evening of Easter day; their last hopes, too, are destroyed. One would have to turn all the Easter stories upside down, if one wanted to present them in the words of Faust: "They are celebrating the resurrection of the Lord, for they themselves are resurrected." No, they are not themselves resurrected. What they experience is fear and doubt, and what only gradually awakens joy and jubilation in their hearts is just this: They, the disciples, on this Easter day, are the ones marked out by death, but the crucified and buried one is alive. Those who have survived him are the dead, and the dead one is the living.

Hence the miracle of the resurrection does not have a satisfactory explanation in the inner nature of the disciples, nor—and this is a quite unbiblical idea—does it have an analogy in the eternal dying and rebirth in nature. . . . It is the resurrected Christ, therefore, who first reveals the mystery of his history and his person, and above all the meaning of his suffering and death. This is movingly told in the story of the disciples of Emmaus (Lk. xxiv. 13ff.), who were joined on their way by the risen Christ, but did not know him. They tell the stranger at their side the terrible tale of their Master, which has disappointed all their hopes; indeed they can even tell the events of Easter morning, but only as a hopeless story, known to everyone except, apparently, this stranger, until he opens his mouth and reveals to them the deep redeeming meaning of the whole story: "O foolish men, and slow of heart to believe all that the prophets have spoken. Was it not necessary that the Christ should suffer these things and enter into his glory?" (xxiv. 25f.). And so he fans the dying flame in their hearts anew, and they are aware of his presence at the evening meal. Truly, even the disciples at Emmaus cannot hold him as they might an earthly travel companion. The risen Christ is not like one of them. He vanishes from them again. But in the words that he speaks to them and in the supper he eats with them, they have the

pledges of his resurrection and presence. Thus they return
to the circle of their brethren as witnesses, and are met
with the joyful, confession from their midst: "The Lord
has risen indeed, and has appeared to Simon." (xxiv. 34)[12]

It is extremely difficult for us to give up our obsession
with facts. The apologetical method with which we learned
our catechism, the passion for precise historical detail which
is characteristic of an empiricist age, and also the extreme
utility of concern about facts as a pretext for evading issues,
all combine to make us want to know exactly how things
occurred on Easter morning. One can see the TV cameras
rolling up with Cosell and Meredith anxiously pacing the
ground outside the tomb. But facts don't produce faith. In
the very nature of things, they cannot. The issue is presented to us not by a TV documentary, but by a fundamental
challenge: are we prepared to believe that God intervened
in history in the person of Jesus? Are we prepared to believe
that the kingdom was vindicated in the face of its enemies?
That really is the issue, and if we are not prepared to make
that leap of faith, then a TV cassette recording showing the
door rolling back and Jesus bounding forth would not make
us one bit more likely to believe.

The real issue is the kingdom and not the resurrection.
The resurrection is the supreme vindication of the kingdom
and the promise that the kingdom will be fulfilled for all
of us. Well, when someone says to me, "I'm not sure that I
can accept the evidence for the physical resurrection of
Jesus," I am afraid that they rather miss the whole point.
One is either prepared to accept the Good News of the
kingdom or not accept it; one either believes that God has
entered into history in the form of loving service and vindicated the strength of his love or one is not going to believe
it. It seems to me that that is where the decision ought to

12 *Ibid.*, pp. 184–85.

be made. Quibbling about the evidence of the resurrection is quite beside the point.

The resurrection, then, is a symbol; to use a word that offends many Catholics, a myth. By myth I do not mean a fable or a fairy story or a legend; I mean an event that represents a greater event. The Easter phenomenon, the early Christians' experience of Jesus as dead and yet once again alive, is a vindication of the kingdom and a symbol of the kingdom's triumph, a symbol that nothing can stop total fulfillment of the kingdom. To get bogged down in one reality and not to face the greater and more ultimate reality which it represents is to miss the point totally.

And yet, the confused traditional Catholic stubbornly argues, "But will I personally rise from the dead?" For this seems to him to be the most critical issue. What is going to happen to him *personally?* There are two different kinds of answers to the question, both of them, one supposes, valid. One is to say that personal concern is completely understandable, that of course we will live again. The other is to say that we know very, very little about the nature and modality of the new life and that we do not put our faith so much in expectation of a literal physical resurrection as we do in God's love, for, after all, it is God's love that is the cause and the new life which is the effect. He has revealed to us His love and promised to us a new life. We believe the love and accept the gift of new life. We commit ourselves to the reality that God did vindicate Jesus against the powers of sin and death and that that vindication was a promise and pledge of our own life. God lives and loves; Jesus lives; and we, too, will live. That is the proper object of our faith. How the Father proposes to go about arranging these things is a matter which we would be much better advised to leave to him instead of agonizing and quibbling over the details.

"My own personal resurrection is at the center of my faith," said one Catholic to me. One supposes that this is

one valid way of putting it. The resurrection is certainly
the central part of our faith, but I think it must be emphasized that it is only a part, a part of a larger and more
comprehensive message, the message of the Good News of
God's love. The resurrection is merely the event that vindi-
cates the message of love. Our proper focus ought to be on
the whole message and not just on the vindicating event.

The message is, in the final analysis, that we shall live.
One either accepts or rejects that message, and all the
factual details in the world cannot command either acceptance or rejection of it. The man stands at the door of
the banquet and says to us, "I was dead and yet I lived;
my Father has raised me from the dead in order to vindicate the invitation that you all should come into the banquet
and live." The critical issue for us, as always, is whether
we want to take the risk of going into the banquet to find
out what it's really like. There's a strange paradox in this
invitation, for it implies that man can decide for himself if
he is to conquer death. If we accept the kingdom, we are
told, then we will live; if we are ready to believe the triumph
of life over death, then in fact we will triumph over death.

In one of the best of the recent theological articles on
death, the Jesuit theologian Ladislaus Boros notes that death
is the "location" of integral decision. Boros' article should
be carefully read by everyone concerned with the existentialist theological approach to death and resurrection. Death
is a "yes saying," the final, definitive acceptance of the
Good News of the kingdom. In that acceptance of the
Good News, man begins to live. Two paragraphs of the
Boros article are worth quoting:

> *Death is the "location" of integral decision.* The absolute
> is "reached" in death. For a person for a "being" which
> has wholly "come to be itself", this "reaching" always means
> meeting—an encounter. A meeting can take place only be-

tween two persons who can express the "I-thou relationship in freedom. In consequence, man as a person is not dis-
solved in death, but on the contrary becomes a "full
person" for the first time. Therefore, the absolute encounter
must be a personal relationship; hence the Absolute itself
is a person. The event proper to death is coexistence with
or rejection of the Absolute Person by a finite person which
has wholly come to be itself. In consequence, death is
a wholly personal and total decision in regard to a personal
God. Hence,

In death man secures (first of all) eternity for himself.
The total realization of the inward man in death is (if it
occurs as affirmation) a wholly personal co-existence of
a finite with the infinite being, a full participation in God.
This participation in love is, however, twofold: On the one
hand, it means that the being of the Other becomes our
own being; on the other hand, it means that we come to
be "ourselves" even more fully. The infinite fullness of the
Absolute cannot be fully assumed or exhausted by any
finite being. This means that the eternity that comes about
in death can be comprehended only as a limitless process
of growth into an ever richer completion. In heaven, everything static and quantitative is transformed into an un-
limited dynamic process advancing into infinity. The world
occurs in its proper form only if and when man, through
his freely given Yes to God, enters heaven.[13]

It is a long, long way from the unshakable conviction of
the apostles that they had experienced Jesus alive once
again to Boros' existentialist terminology, but both the narration stories in the New Testament and Boros' theorizing
are an attempt to capture in words an incredible experience
and a conviction about the meaning of that experience. The
Really Real is Love; so powerful, generous, and determined

[13] Ladislaus Boros, "Has Life A Meaning?" *Concilium: Immortality and
Resurrection, op. cit.,* p. 17.

a Love that nothing can contain it, not even sin and death; and so resourceful a Love that we, too, will live.

The message is the same as it always was, no more easy to believe now than it was when Jesus appeared on the scene and confidently asserted that both he and the kingdom he was preaching would be vindicated. The early Church does not portray its leaders as brave, heroic men, gratefully accepting a vindication about which they were confident. Quite the contrary, it portrays them as not wanting to believe, not wanting to accept the possibility of vindication, but being so overwhelmed by the experience of vindication, they believed in spite of themselves. If we are to believe, we too will believe in spite of ourselves.

CHAPTER 12

THE FUTURE AND THE CHURCH

More ink has been spilled on the subject of "eschatology" in the last seventy years than on any other subject in Christian theology. Jesus preached an eschaton, that is to say, the beginning of a new age marked by a special intervention of God. But, to oversimplify the matter somewhat, the critical question is, when does the eschaton begin? Albert Schweitzer, one of the giants of the early phases of Scripture scholarship in this century, was convinced that Jesus expected the eschaton in the very near future. He was essentially a prophet of the coming of the Last Days and therefore had no thought of a long interval between his death and the beginning of the Last Days or of founding a permanent community.

Schweitzer's influence has been pervasive, and I suppose is still very much a part of the pop theology. But in the 1930's, the brilliant British scholar C. H. Dodd reanalyzed the question of the eschaton and the Last Days and concluded that instead of Schweitzer's "consequent eschatology" Jesus was really preaching "realized eschatology"; that is to say, an eschaton that had already come and was already manifested in his own words and deeds. Even though Dodd's position does not receive the wide popular acceptance of Schweitzer's, the British scholar has by far the better argument, since recent criticism has demonstrated pretty conclusively that most of the passages on which Schweitzer bases his arguments for consequent eschatology are in fact "not authentic"; that is, they are certainly the work of the writers of the New Testament and not of Jesus himself.

The most recent scholarship tends to emphasize an opinion which is a combination of Schweitzer and Dodd, observing that sometimes Jesus spoke of the eschaton as though it had already arrived and at other times as though it were still in the future—an eschatology that is both realized and consequent, that is here present and yet to come. This position, summarized in A. L. Moore's book, *The Coming of the Kingdom,* represents a curious swing of the circle because it brings us back by an immense amount of exegetical and religious sophistication to a position which was prominent enough before Schweitzer. Moore summarizes the position of Jesus' understanding of the future by saying that it is based on twin themes—eschatology and grace. Jesus is sure that the End, being the revelation of his person at work and the end of all ambiguity and contradiction, is near. "On the other hand, he is also convinced that God will allow men time for the event of life and the grace and comfort of His Holy Spirit. Time, that is, to enter into the significance of Christ's work, to exercise faith, hope, and love."[1]

There is not much doubt that many in the early Church expected an early fulfillment of the kingdom. By the time St. Luke wrote his gospel, the "official position" was shifting against such an expectation, but the careful studies of scholars like Moore and Norman Perrin provide no evidence that Jesus himself either encouraged or expected an imminent vindication. Jesus was more concerned about the urgency of the present situation than he was about the future. That concern came not so much from his expectation that time would run out, though he insisted that it would, but rather

[1] A. L. Moore, *The Coming of the Kingdom.* Leiden: E. J. Brill, 1966, p. 206.

from the immensity of the opportunity and challenge that it offered. Perrin remarks, ". . . almost all the elements in the tradition which give definite *form* to the future expectation in the teaching of Jesus fail the test of authenticity."[2] Perrin notes that the apocalyptic expectation in Mark 13 is certainly a work of the early Christians, and yet the expectation of the Parousia in Matthew is a development of the Son of Man tradition, and that in turn is an early Christian interpretation of the resurrection. Equally spectacular, notes Perrin, is the way in which sayings that express its imminent expectation fail to stand up to serious investigation. The only elements that can be traced back to Jesus with any degree of certainty are the most general expectations of vindication and judgment. "These express confidence in *a* vindication, but they tell us nothing about its form. The difference between this and the general expectations of the first century, both Jewish and Christian, is spectacular."[3]

Many writers are inclined to attribute authenticity to Jesus' denial that he knew the date of the Final End. Although such an assertion would have fit in very well with the shifting position of the official church after the fall of Jerusalem, these scholars are still skeptical that any early Christian writer would dare to put such an expression in the mouth of Jesus. So scandalous a saying would not have been tolerated if the tradition did not very strongly assert that Jesus very clearly said something along those lines.

This whole examination of the eschatology question leans far more toward the position of C. H. Dodd than that of Schweitzer. The kingdom of God is present, not completely perhaps, but it is present. The present time is filled with the reality of God. Nothing more is to be expected than a complete fulfillment of that experience in the future. The reality is now known incompletely, ambiguously, immersed in conflict and temptation. Clarity and victory are yet to

2 Norman Perrin, *Rediscovering the Teaching of Jesus.* New York: Harper & Row, 1967, p. 203.
3 *Ibid.,* p. 203.

come. The apostle lives in the era of Now but also of the Not Yet. The table fellowship they share is of the kingdom, but it is also an anticipation of a superior fellowship which is yet to come. The future is already present but not completely so.

Perhaps part of our difficulty in understanding this mystery of the eschaton Present and Yet to Come is that we are dealing with a mode of viewing time which is very foreign to our present Western time sense. It also is very likely foreign to the time sense of the early Christians who could not conceive of a vindication in which the resurrection and the final consummation of things would be long separated. Exactly how long Jesus personally estimated the "time of grace" would be is not known, because he apparently avoided making any comment on that subject. His sense of urgency, let it be repeated, is not rooted in the expectation that the end will come next week but rather in the importance of his message. The message is so important, the opportunity is so great, that it almost does not matter when the end will in fact come. One can be quite certain that if Jesus were told that it would be thousands of years and hence that his invitation was not quite as urgent as he made it, he would have been quite surprised, for the urgency of the announcement of the kingdom and the invitation to the banquet were quite independent of how long it would be before the doors of the banquet hall were closed.

But even the early Christians could not separate their sense of urgency from the consideration of measured time. Their solution was to conclude that the time obviously had to be very brief. Our conclusion is that it will be a long time and, hence, there is nothing to get excited about. Jesus' point was that time was irrelevant and that there was plenty to be excited about because the kingdom of his Father was near, indeed, even among us. But, like every other element of his challenging message, the near presence of the kingdom can easily be evaded. We who are his followers will announce that we are about to change our lives, that we are about to begin our *metanoia*, about to respond to his expectations, but then we adjust the pace of our change and the speed of our *metanoia* so that we are guaranteed that even if Jesus should not reappear on the scene for half a million years we still would be too late. Our *metanoia* is under way, but at a rate which makes it absolutely certain that we will never finish. When the End does come, whenever that is, we will have the perfect excuse: "If only you gave us a little bit more time."

The phony urgency of the early Christians—phony because it had to rely on the false expectation of imminent end—is surely more attractive than our apathetic indifference. They at least had a sense of urgency and one sees very little of that among contemporary Christians. Why hurry, there still is plenty of time, we tell each other, and when the man at the door of the wedding banquet says, "Make haste, the kingdom of my Father is at hand," we say, "But you've been telling us that for a couple of millennia; what's all the rush?"

One imagines that the picture must be seen from his viewpoint to understand what all the rush is. There is of course a rather finite amount of time in the lives of each one of us, but, even more important, the point of Jesus' message is that the magnificent opportunity of the kingdom is present for us, at least inchoately, here and now. We are absolute fools to overlook that opportunity. We are cheating ourselves; we are being blind, deaf, stupid, and insensitive. And we cheerfully acknowledge all these accusations and say, "Not just now, Lord; I still have to go out and try my new yoke of oxen. You wait here at the door and tomorrow or the next day at the latest I'll be back, and then I'll come in and see what this party of yours is all about."

The time between the Now and the Not Yet is the time of the Church. The Church is a community of those who are standing ready for the coming of the Lord who continue to proclaim the message of the Good News, however inadequately and halfheartedly. It is an assembly of those who take the message of Jesus of Nazareth seriously and have confidence in the vindication of that message in the resurrection of Jesus. With characteristic grace, Gunther Bornkamm describes its urgency:

> But this very community who await the coming Lord and, in the spirit, are already certain of his presence, bind themselves consciously, at the same time, to the way and the message of the earthly Jesus, and take his orders and promise as a guide for their own earthly way; not in spite of their hopes which are fixed on the future, but precisely because of them. Their expectation of the coming of the Lord gains its power and its reason for existence in their knowledge of past and present. From now on the great theme of the early Christian mission is the proclamation and delivery of the message of the redemption, which happened through the cross and the resurrection, and the kingship of Jesus Christ over the world.[4]

As I remarked in an earlier chapter, it may not be much of a Church, but it is the only one we have. It has made a rather serious mess of its mission of continuing the proclamation of the Good News. Not very many of its members are lights on the mountaintop or salt of the earth or leaven amid the dough, and not many of its leaders correspond to the ideal model of discipleship as presented in the gospel. But for all its faults, the Church is the only institution in the world that even claims to be continuing the proclamation of the Good News and to be anticipating the fulfillment

[4] Bornkamm, *op. cit.*, p. 188.

of the wedding banquet. I suppose, without wishing to get involved in the whole vast theological debate, that, in the final analysis, this is what the infallibility of the Church means. Despite all the frailty of its leadership, all the evasions of its membership, all the incredible mistakes it has made, the Church still continues, however obscurely and inadequately, to preach the Good News and will, if Jesus' confidence of vindication is to be justified, continue to preach the kingdom until the fullness of the kingdom is achieved.

Railings against the failure of the Church ought to be seen from the perspective we have taken in this book as an utter waste of time. To be angry at the inadequacy of the Church or the pettiness and the occasional corruption of Church leaders may be a superb way of working out the emotional conflicts of our childhood, but it has nothing to do with responding to the message of the kingdom, with attending the wedding banquet, or with living the lives of festive joy to which we are called. Nor has anger anything to do with the proclamation of the Good News of the kingdom. Some anger is perhaps justified, and certainly efforts at improving the human organization of the Church are most praiseworthy, but anger has to be transcended, and organizational renewal, however necessary, does not by itself guarantee the more effective proclamation of the kingdom or more enthusiastic acceptance of it.

Yet contemporary Catholics are obsessed by institutional forms and class-conflict themes in the life of the Church. There are some laymen, for example, whose major religious activity seems to be focused on the insistence that ecclesiastical financial records be made public. I would be inclined to think that the records ought to be public, too, though whether they are or not is rather unimportant compared with the message of the kingdom. Some priests will speak of little more than the need for collegiality or co-responsibility among the priests of the diocese and for the election of bishops by priests, and perhaps people, too. Now I myself am a convinced democrat. I do not believe that we are likely to have reform in the Church or decent leadership until we return to the traditional means of selecting our bishops—that is to say, election. But yet from many of these democratic enthusiasts I hear very little about the Good News and practically nothing about the wedding banquet that's going on. The plea for democracy has replaced the proclamation and this I think is a grave misfortune, because even when we become democratically organized—as we most certainly will—we will not necessarily be any more likely to proclaim the kingdom then than we are now, not unless we go through a *metanoia* by which we understand that democratization is a means and not an end. A democratic Church would be less inadequate as a herald of the Good News than a corrupt and authoritarian one, but democracy is by itself no guarantee that we will become excited once again about the nearness of the kingdom of God.

One way Jesus could have guaranteed that his community of followers would have been adequate to his task would be to exclude all human beings from its membership. A group of specially trained, highly disciplined archangels could have pulled it off brilliantly—at least, for all we know about archangels they could have pulled it off. It may well be that they are as inept as we are.

But once he committed himself to operating with human beings, Jesus was bound to get in trouble. Presumably he knew this, and if he didn't he discovered it very early in his dealings with his disciples. Yet, as we noted earlier in the chapter on hope, Jesus seemed to exult in the weakness and frailty of his methods. He would not underwrite the kingdom by producing at the appropriate moment twelve legions of angels, for that would be to rely on power, earthly power, even though supernatural in its origins. And if we would not ultimately make the guarantee of his kingdom by the appearance of the angelic shock troops, neither would he have it rest ultimately on the most brilliant and charismatic of leaders. For the power of charismatic leaders is also finally an earthly power, and to rely on such power for vindication would be to prove false Jesus' basic theme that the power of the kingdom came not from earth but from God.

Jesus certainly does not reject charismatic leaders and, on the whole, the Church has some reason to be proud of the great men it has produced. But its ultimate vindication will take place quite independently of our charisma, although, in some way we do not fully understand, our charisma is also necessary to prepare the groundwork. Those who persist in judging the message of Jesus by the membership and leadership of his Church are setting up criterion which he explicitly rejected beforehand and whose validity collapses in the face of Jesus' decision to call fragile human beings to be his followers and also to exult in their fragility.

The Church is primarily a local community, or, as the current theologians say, the whole Church is manifested in the local community but not completely contained within it. In another book[5] I will discuss this paradox at some length. It is sufficient here to observe that the table fellowship, which is at the core of the Christian's anticipatory experience of the heavenly banquet, is necessarily something that is celebrated locally and with a small group of people. The kingdom of God is present in the world most specifically and most specially when a small group of the followers of Jesus band together to share the fellowship of the Eucharistic banquet. But the banquet is a world-wide phenomenon even though it is celebrated only in specific loci. Our little band of brothers, eating on our "location," are nonetheless a part of the world-wide banquet, and we are held together with one another by the common banquet, the common

[5] Andrew M. Greeley, *What a Modern Catholic Believes about the Church.* Chicago: Thomas More Press, 1972.

faith, the common expectation of the ultimate vindication of Jesus and the kingdom, and our common commitment to proclaiming both by our life and by our words the Good News of the message of Jesus. Just as the early community had a leadership, we have leadership whose principal job is to devote all their energies to the explicit proclamation of the kingdom, and by so doing to prevent the rest of us from taking our eyes off that goal and to begin to live in such a way that we become like the light of the world and the salt of the earth.

These are the essential things about the Church. Most of the rest is historical development which is important, valuable, and worthy of our reverence and respect. The forms evolved through the centuries are not to be lightly cast aside, especially not because immature and uneducated enthusiasts think they are irrelevant. But neither are these forms to be confused with the essentials. Yet, despite the overwhelming evidence in the New Testament about what is essential and what is not, we still manage to make the essential accidental and the accidental essential. The reason is, I suspect, that we want to, that such confusion simplifies our lives immensely because it evades the challenge.

The Roman Congregation of the Clergy, for example, may be as important as some of its supporters and administrators think it is, or it may be as inept and misguided as many of its critics think it is, but in the strict sense of the word it is irrelevant in terms of the ultimate message. The Congregation of the Clergy cannot guarantee the effective proclamation of the kingdom, much less can it guarantee men's response to the kingdom, but neither can it prevent us from preaching the kingdom. Its mistakes and ineptitudes are no excuse for our not responding to the invitation of the kingdom. The best it can do is to facilitate somewhat the preaching of the kingdom, but it is, from the point of view of the proclamation of the kingdom, a trivial institution—however immensely dignified its membership may be. Because the Congregation is trivial does not mean that it should not exist, just that neither its supporters nor its critics should permit themselves to be obsessed by it.

And yet it is so splendid to concentrate on means and ignore ends; indeed, after a while we get really skillful at it. Our whole lives become a concern over means. That is, of course, the way to build a fully human, open, authentic, honest style of life, a life which is so concerned about means that even to the last it refuses a final, determinative decision about the End.

Jesus had some rather nasty words to say about that kind of life, words that spoke of exterior darkness and weeping and gnashing of teeth.

CHAPTER 13

JESUS AND POLITICAL ACTION

The reader is probably conscious that I have engaged in dialogue in two directions in this book. On the one hand, I am speaking to those who confuse the part for the whole, who turn away from the very fundamental simple message of Good News that Jesus proclaimed to concern themselves with theological details, organizational structures, or historical verifications. On the other hand, I am engaged with, or perhaps against, those who attempt to reduce the gospel to a program for radical political action. Neither of these responses to Jesus' message is so very new. The former is the course of the Pharisees, the latter is the course of the Zealots. In more recent years the Zealot temptation has reappeared with a good deal of seductiveness. The temptation is all the more attractive because the charge for which Jesus was executed was pretty clearly one of Zealotry; he did have some criticism of the existing world in common with them. But Zealotry as a temptation is not to be more radical than Jesus, but to be less radical.

Let me make it clear that my abhorrence of the Zealot temptation, particularly as it is manifested in much of the current "theology of revolution," has nothing to do with the conviction that Christians should stay out of political and social action. As long as I can remember I have been a political and social activist and still am even though I do not burn draft records or march on picket lines. I do not engage in these activities because I am opposed to counterproductive methods of social action. I was an activist long before many of our contemporary fashionable activists, and I suspect I will continue to be one long after they have given up on it and marched off into the desert to await the inevitable eschatological greening of America.

I object to the theology of revolution on two counts: (1) as a social scientist and (2) as a Christian. The latter objection is perhaps more pertinent to this book, but let me take up the social science objection first so as to clear it away.

The call for revolution is usually based on the assumption that the present disorder is the result of malice, selfishness, the concentration of power, and the maldistribution of wealth. The malicious and selfish men are to be swept out of power. If power and wealth are redistributed, then injustice will be substantially reduced if not eliminated and the world will be a better place. The oppressed and the suffering of the earth, in other words, are to be delivered from their oppression and suffering by seizing power and redistributing the goods of the world.

Such an analysis has the appeal of simplicity and clarity. One knows both what must be done and what the effects will be. What the appeal lacks is any understanding of history or of economics or of human society.

If one looks at the so-called underdeveloped nations with any kind of economic sophistication, one has to say that the redistribution of power or wealth is not likely to have much impact on the society in those countries. New models of social organization, acquiring of industrial skills, and drastic economic changes are the only things that will improve the lot of the people in these countries. The passion for political revolution is a marvelous outlet for anger, but it does not necessarily solve the problems of economic and social structure.

We are also told that it is intolerable that a small proportion of the world's population controls most of its wealth and a large proportion lives in poverty. I am willing to agree that it is intolerable, but I do not agree that the poverty can be eliminated by taking goods away from the wealthy of the world and giving them to the poor. Problems of international production and distribution are, alas, far more complicated. The harsh truth is that we do not know yet how to solve most of these problems, but redistribution of goods, however much it appeals to the simple-minded enthusiast, would only have marginal impact on eliminating poverty from the earth.

Quite apart from the fact that enthusiasts for revolution are quite innocent of any social and economic and technological sophistication, there also is the overwhelming evidence that revolutions do not work. As George Orwell said in a quote we noted earlier, all revolutions fail, but not all the failures are the same. Those American liberals, Christian and non-Christian who are enthusiastic apostles of revolution, have for the last half century waxed optimistic about first the Russian, then the Chinese, and now the Cuban revolutions. Evidence is overwhelming that in each instance economic progress was slowed down rather than accelerated by the revolution. The American radicals, somehow or other, have their moral aestheticism more satisfied by the drab gray dullness of Castro's Cuba than by the corruption of Batista's Cuba. Recently, even they have begun to admit that, despite the vast amount of Russian money that has been poured in, the Cuban economy is not much better than it was fifteen years ago.

And one need only note the unending series of revolutions in Latin America to realize that, while the elite holding power may change, the elites still govern pretty much on their own authority without widespread social assent for their own benefit and profit. There is still the pious myth that a Marxist elite will somehow or other promote social and economic progress. But even a small amount of information about the economic and social problems of the underdeveloped countries indicates that what is needed is not a new power elite but rather new methods of and attitudes toward production and distribution of goods and, in many instances, more effective means of population control.

I am not saying that some governments are not oppressive; clearly they are, and perhaps the only justification for revolution is the removal of oppressive and unrepresentative governments. If the revolutionary goals are limited to that, the revolution is likely to be moderately successful (as in America). But if it attempts to remake the social structure and to eliminate suffering and misery by redistributing power, there is no reason in the world to expect success and every reason—historically, economically, and sociologically—to expect failure. It may be much more romantic and dramatic to advocate revolution than to promote economic development; just the same, if one is really interested in improving the human condition, economic development is far more important.

When I try to explain this position to some of the Catholic revolutionaries, their response is, "You may be right but the people won't wait." One is not sure whom they mean by "the people." When some intellectuals in underdeveloped countries, a handful of students, and a handfull of nonrepresentative members of minority groups in the United States cry out, "All power to the people," they are hilarious. If the people really had power unrestrained by the government and the judicial system, they would promptly clap the revolutionaries into jail.

In a world where the problems are as complex and intricate as our own, about all that revolution can accomplish is political liberation. Many of those who are most enthusiastic about a theology of revolution seem to be responding to what they consider to be the scandalous identification of the Church with the Establishment. That certain ecclesiastical leaders have become too closely involved with those who possess political power I have no doubt. I am skeptical as to whether replacing one set of political leaders with another really does much to change the structure of society, and while I can understand anger and impatience with those ecclesiastics and self-announced Christians who stand in the way of social progress and change, I do not think the solution lies in blasting them out of their positions of power, satisfying as such an exercise might be. I do not think that anger at reactionaries and "fat cats" represents the specifically Christian response to human social problems.

Jesus was a radical, make no mistake about that. As Oscar Cullmann points out in his book, *Jesus and the Revolutionaries*, he was an eschatological radical. He criticized the existing order but he rejected political movements as the important means of transforming the world order, because political movements ". . . divert one's attention from the kingdom of God . . . and violate by their use of violence the command to absolute justice and absolute love."[1]

Cullmann summarizes his careful examination of Jesus' relationship with the Zealots in the following fashion:

> The eschatological radicalism of Jesus, as we have seen, underlies his absolute obedience to the will of God and the resulting condemnation of legalism, hypocrisy, and injustice. The Zealots also proceed from an eschatological radicalism; but Jesus is much more radical not only with respect to his concept of the kingdom of God, but also

[1] Oscar Cullmann, *Jesus and the Revolutionaries*. New York: Harper & Row, 1970, pp. 51–52.

with respect to his application of normas. His goal and norms are "not of this world," as is the case of the Zealots. For this reason he directs his criticism not only against the defenders of the existing order, but also against the Zealots. That does not infer that it is Jesus' intention that we should in general eliminate our ethical judgment by indiscriminately including all in the same criticism. I have vigorously stressed that Jesus found himself in a certain sense close to the Zealots—as also to the Pharisees. There was for him a Zealotist temptation. But exactly for that reason he warned those to whom he found himself close of the terrible consequences of their fundamental position, which made all their efforts so questionable and ultimately caused them to be transformed from nonconformists into conformists. Their resistance became indeed finally so popular in Palestine that it required courage to criticize them for not taking their norms from the kingdom which is not of this world.[2]

There are then two points in Jesus' program for remaking the world: (1) Man must first accept the kingdom, and (2) man must act according to the norms of justice and love. This is not an escape from political activism, though in Jesus' time the implications of justice and love and for the reorganization and society were not nearly as clear or well developed as they are today. Indeed, one might even say more. Under the impulse of the ethic of justice and love which Jesus preached we have become far more conscious of what the good society ought to be like. What Jesus is saying, rather, is that unless men are prepared to commit themselves to the vision of God's love for us that he has come to preach then they will not be able to love one another. One generation's revolutionaries can turn into the next generation's oppressors. Anyone who knows much history can have no doubt about that, but

[2] Cullmann, *ibid.*, pp. 57–58.

the argument still remains: Will the plan of Jesus work? Will the conversion to the kingdom of God and the consequent willingness to live by justice and love really transform, or at least notably improve the human condition, even before the complete fulfillment of the kingdom?

I suppose the only answer to that question is that empirically we do not know because the program of Jesus has never been tried.

Revolutions, even violent revolutions, may occasionally be necessary, but they are, at best, risky affairs, and if there is not something more involved than just the redistribution of power and attempted redistribution of wealth, the historical record is clear: the revolution will fail, and may even make things worse instead of better. Jesus did not so much call for the end of revolutions as he called on men to understand that the revolution was a pathetically inadequate means of transforming the human condition and that that condition would be transformed only when men had enough confidence in God's love for them to be willing to take the great risk of loving one another.

It can be objected that in my view of things social change will necessarily be a slow and gradual process and that "the people won't wait." But of course the people will wait and are going to have to wait. If my method is somewhat slower, it is also more likely to be effective. I suspect sometimes that the Christian radicals want success because they realize in their heart of hearts that if they don't have dramatic and rapid success they will lose their enthusiasm. The point is, however, that the Christian by definition is not supposed to lose. His faith in the coming of the kingdom does not excuse him from commitment to the world. On the contrary, it holds him both more firmly and more confidently in his commitment to the world, more firmly because he knows that he has no choice but to love, and more confidently because he knows that in the end love will be vindicated.

I cannot insist too strongly at this point that the Christian is not running away from social problems. He is not waiting for an eschatological kingdom where all will be well. He rather believes that his commitment to the eschatological kingdom tells him to practice love in all his relationships. He has always believed this, but the modern Christian, in addition, perceives the vast social implications of love. He also understands that in some way or other his exercise of love in the social order both proclaims the kingdom and also prepares for—though it does not cause —its fulfillment. He does not, he cannot give up and retreat to some rural commune, but neither can he attempt to short-circuit the process by falling back on hatred and violence. He does not abhor political action. He does not despise politics. He is not even afraid of amassing political power, though he knows that the most that power can do is modify structures to an extent that love becomes feasible; it does not create love, and in the absence of love social reforms have minimum effectiveness.

The eschatological vision does not mean that the Christian is opposed to school desegragation, for example. Quite the contrary, he enthusiastically supports it. He realizes that in the final analysis tension between black and white will be resolved only when there is more love between the two. Equalized power can prevent injustice and may give people opportunity to become fully human. It can even create a situation where love can be possible.

The Christian realizes that he must commit himself to both equalized power and love without ever having the slightest thought of withdrawing that commitment. He cannot therefore engage in demonstrations or revolutionary acts or liturgical gestures and then withdraw from the field with the rather soreheaded complaint that it didn't do any good. Neither can he succumb to the temptation of thinking that he can force men to be virtuous. He may be able to prevent them from abusing others by power and law, but the Christian realizes that you teach men to love only by loving yourself.

There isn't much doubt, after one has read a book like Cullmann's, that this is where "Jesus was at." The Zealots dismissed him as a pious dreamer, the Pharisees dismissed him as a violator of the law, the Establishment viewed him as a dangerous radical, and so the Romans disposed of him—or at least tried to. One has the appalling feeling that his political and social message, would receive the same response today. The realists would think it naïve; the defenders of the status quo would think it revolutionary. And yet Jesus was neither a naïve person nor a revolutionary, at least as the word is normally understood; so once again, he was misunderstood and once again, one suspects, deliberately. It is too bad because his plan at least deserves a try, and save on a small scale with tiny groups of human beings, it never really has been tried. It is a revolution that is ultimately not of this world at all, yet one that claims to transform this world too. It is a revolution which begins, curiously enough, with an invitation to a banquet, and if we ever go through the portals of the banquet hall we will find the revolutionary leader beginning the conversation with, "I suppose you wonder why I've called you all together."

CHAPTER 14

CONCLUSION

In one of the more splendid "Star Trek" episodes the *Enterprise* and her crew come to a planet which combines first-century Rome and twentieth-century America in its culture. Caesar's proconsul presses Kirk, McCoy, and the pointy-eared Spock into service as gladiators. After the usual number of close calls the officers of the *Enterprise* are saved (at the cost of his life) by a huge gentle gladiator named Flavius. He preaches universal brotherhood and seems to worship the sun. When they have "beamed" back to their starship, the three heroes muse over Flavius, puzzled by his worship of the sun. Uhura, the lovely black communications officer, tells them they have misunderstood Flavius: it is not the "sun" he worshiped but the "Son."

"Interesting, even fascinating," says Spock. "Christ and Caesar—they have them both here even as earth did."

"And Christ is triumphing over Caesar just as he did on earth," murmers Kirk. "It's happening once more. Wouldn't it be marvelous to be able to watch it again?"

Mr. Chekov is instructed to take the *Enterprise* out of orbit, and at warp factor 2 it proceeds on its pilgrimage through space.

"Star Trek"—and may the Lord forgive the networks for killing it—was the closest thing to an explicit morality play that the idiot tube has ever produced. But this particular episode was one that ought to have stopped every Christian short. We might be tempted to ask, in the words of Alice Meynell's great poem, ". . . in what guise He trod the Pleiades . . ."?

> But in the eternities
> Doubtless we shall compare together, hear
> A million alien Gospels, in what guise
> He trod the Pleiades, the Lyre, the Bear.[1]

Whether he trod the Pleiades or not we do not know. We have at least left behind the ethnocentrism (or perhaps one should say cosmocentrism) of those theologians who argued that it was impossible for the Incarnation to occur on any other planet. It is entirely possible that some future counterpart of the *Enterprise* will encounter somewhere in the universe other life forms to whom the Father has manifested His love. We could no more legitimately object to that than the citizens of Nazareth could object to the Father manifesting His love to the Samaritans. From what Jesus has told us of his Father, we would find it difficult to see how He could avoid getting involved with whatever other stray life forms are to be found out there among the galaxies. If He managed to fall in love with us, if He could be insanely generous with such rather low level life forms as we, how could He not love whatever life should appear in the universe?

It would be interesting to know what He thinks of the Vulcans.

But the important point is not whether Jesus walks in the Pleiades; it is that he walked here on earth. Captain

[1] Alice Meynell, "Christ in the Universe," *The Golden Book of Catholic Poetry,* edited by Alfred Noyes. Philadelphia and New York: J. B. Lippincott Company, 1964, p. 234.

Kirk and the crew of the *Enterprise* might well envy Flavius
and his friends for the chance to be part of it all again.
But we are part of it now—or we can be if we want to.
Our pilgrimage does not take us through physical space
like the *Enterprise,* but it is a pilgrimage just the same
—a pilgrimage of the human spirit in its restless quest for
the Absolute. Jesus is not merely a manifestation of the
Absolute; he is simultaneously the assurance that the Absolute loves us and a guide on the pilgrimage.

The issue is the same for us as it has been for all our
predecessors: Do we want to go on the pilgrimage? Do we
wish to trust the Absolute? Do we believe the claim of
Jesus to be a guide for the pilgrimage? The *Enterprise*
moving at warp factor 2, the Israelites following Moses out
into the desert, our accepting the invitation to the wedding
feast—all manifest a fundamental trust in the graciousness
of being, without which pilgrimage becomes impossible.
The challenge of Jesus may not be "relevant," but demanding its acceptance has always been and always will be.

In his discussion of religious symbols Paul Ricoeur speaks
of the "first" and "second naivete." In the "first naivete"
man accepts his religious symbols in a simple, unself-con-
scious way. He does not need to reflect, to analyze, to
explain, to interpret—at least he does not need much of
these activities. Such a "naive faith" has been characteristic
of most believers in most periods of human history; the
Breton fisherman or the Irish washerwoman of pious legend
had this sort of faith. So perhaps did our parents and
our grandparents, maybe even some of our teachers. It is
fashionable in some circles to ridicule "naive faith"; but
such ridicule is merely a display of shallow pseudosophis-
tication.

But however admirable the "first naivete" may be, it is
not possible for an increasing number of us. We do not
simply repeat sacred poetry, we must analyze it, take it
apart, interpret it, uncover the various levels of narration

and meaning. We are products of an analytic, scientific age, and our myths and poems must be analyzed. We must know what the symbol means.

There is nothing wrong with that. The ability to analyze is one of man's most impressive accomplishments. But can we go beyond analysis? Or do we become like the English professor who is so sophisticated in taking apart the poetry of the Bard that he no longer can enjoy Shakespeare's vision? He can tell us what every word in a line means, but he can no longer thrill at the thought of Juliet as the sun. He has learned prose so well that he can no longer speak or listen to poetry.

I can almost hear some readers say, "But is Jesus real, or is he just poetry?" The only answer is that poetry is more real than prose. Jesus is real precisely because he is poetry, precisely because his life and message are symbols —symbols of God's love for us.

In the second naivete, having achieved a more sensitive and profound understanding of the meaning of the symbol, we give ourselves over to it once again and now the symbol has even more power for us than it did before. The poetry expert who has gone beyond analysis can take even more delight in Juliet as the sun because he has explored all the implications of the image.

A man still hung up on prose says skeptically, "But of course Juliet really isn't the sun, is she?" How badly he misses the point. The whole message of the image is not that she is something less than the real sun, but rather for one who loves her she is something much more. The poetic image is never an exaggeration of reality, it is an understatement of it.

We live in an age of prose. As a race we have left behind the first naivete and have not yet quite made it to the second. We tear our symbols apart and then sorrowfully view the pieces, lamenting that we have wrecked our myths. For prosaic Christians, this age of analysis is one more marvelous excuse. Obviously, we don't have to wonder about whether we ought to accept the invitation to the wedding banquet. After all, the wedding feast is "only a symbol."

This has been largely a book of prose; a book of pilgrimage, perhaps, between the first and the second naivetes. I have "taken apart" the person and the message of Jesus, analyzed, interpreted, and explained. Such an effort is not a foolish one. It is absolutely necessary for men of our time to engage in such a prosaic task. But the critical question for me and for the reader is: Now that we have "explained" Jesus, what do we do about him?

Are we or are we not going to that wedding feast?